UNCORRECTED PROOF

AL CAPONE
SHINES MY SHOES

Gennifer Choldenko

September 2009

$16.99 ($21.00 CAN)

Fiction

Ages 10 up   Grades 5 up

288 pages

978-0-8037-3460-9

Dial Books for Young Readers
New York

AL CAPONE
SHINES MY
SHOES

Al Capone Shines My Shoes

Gennifer Choldenko

Dial Books for Young Readers

Dial Books for Young Readers [colophon]
DIAL BOOKS FOR YOUNG READERS
A division of Penguin Young Readers Group
Published by The Penguin Group
Penguin Group (USA) Inc., 375 Hudson Street, New York, NY 10014, U.S.A.
Penguin Group (Canada), 90 Eglinton Avenue East, Suite 700, Toronto, Ontario, Canada M4P 2Y3
(a division of Pearson Penguin Canada Inc.)
Penguin Books Ltd, 80 Strand, London WC2R 0RL, England
Penguin Ireland, 25 St. Stephen's Green, Dublin 2, Ireland (a division of Penguin Books Ltd)
Penguin Group (Australia), 250 Camberwell Road, Camberwell, Victoria 3124, Australia
(a division of Pearson Australia Group Pty Ltd)
Penguin Books India Pvt Ltd, 11 Community Centre, Panchsheel Park, New Delhi - 110 017, India
Penguin Group (NZ), 67 Apollo Drive, Rosedale, North Shore 0632, New Zealand
(a division of Pearson New Zealand Ltd)
Penguin Books (South Africa) (Pty) Ltd, 24 Sturdee Avenue, Rosebank,
Johannesburg 2196, South Africa
Penguin Books Ltd, Registered Offices: 80 Strand, London WC2R 0RL, England

1 3 5 7 9 10 8 6 4 2

This is a work of fiction. All names, characters, places, organizations, and events portrayed
in this book are products of the author's imagination or are used fictitiously to lend a
sense of realism to the story.

CIP info T/K

To my brother,
GREY CATTELL JOHNSON,
who is every bit as kind as Moose

TABLE OF CONTENTS

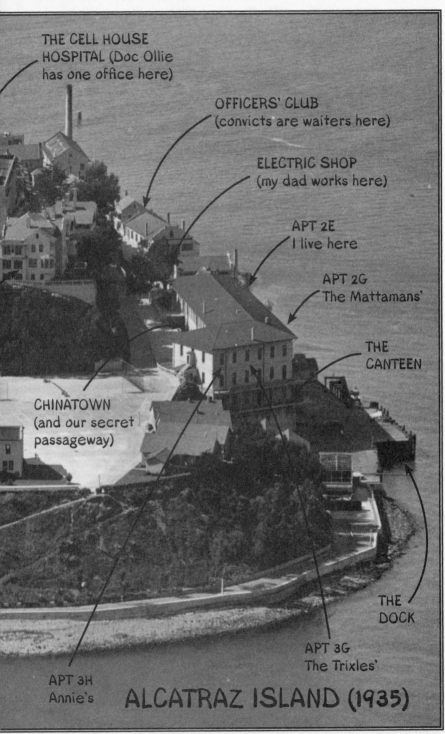

THE CELL HOUSE
HOSPITAL (Doc Ollie
has one office here)

OFFICERS' CLUB
(convicts are waiters here)

ELECTRIC SHOP
(my dad works here)

APT 2E
I live here

APT 2G
The Mattamans'

THE
CANTEEN

CHINATOWN
(and our secret
passageway)

APT 3H
Annie's

APT 3G
The Trixles'

THE
DOCK

ALCATRAZ ISLAND (1935)

1. THE CREAM OF THE CRIMINAL CROP

▪ ▪

Monday, August 5, 1935

Nothing is the way it's supposed to be when you live on an island with a billion birds, a ton of bird crap, a few dozen rifles, machine guns, and automatics, and 278 of America's worst criminals—"the cream of the criminal crop" as one of our felons likes to say. The convicts on Alcatraz are rotten to the core, crazy in the head, and as slippery as eels in axle grease.

And then there's me. Moose Flanagan. I live on Alcatraz along with twenty-four other kids and one more on the way. My father works as a prison guard and an electrician in the cell house up top. I live where most of us "civilians" do, in 64 building, which is dockside on the east side of Alcatraz—a base hit from the mobster Al Capone.

Not many twelve-year-old boys can say that. Not many kids can say that when their toilet is stopped up, they get Seven Fingers, the ax murderer, to help them out, either. Even simple things are upside down and backwards here. Take getting my socks washed. Every Wednesday we put out our dirty laundry in big white bags marked with our name: FLANAGAN. Every Monday our clothes come back starched, pressed, folded, and smelling of soap and flour. They look like my mom washed them for me.

Except she didn't.

My laundry man is Alcatraz #85: Al Capone. He has help, of course. Machine Gun Kelly works right alongside him in the laundry along with thirty other no-name hit men, con men, mad dog murderers, and a handful of bank robbers too.

They do a good job washing the clothes for us and most everyone else on the island. But sometimes they do a little extra.

The cons don't care for Officer Trixle, so his laundry doesn't return the same way as everyone else's. His shirts are missing buttons, underwear is stiff with starch or dyed pansy pink, pants are missing a cuff or the fly is sewn shut so the guy can't even take a leak unless he pulls his pants down like a little girl.

I can't say the cons are wrong about Officer Trixle. Darby Trixle is the kind of guy who only his wife likes—and not that much either. Last Saturday my best friend Jimmy Mattaman and I were looking for a barrel for Jimmy's fly menagerie, and Janet Trixle, Darby's seven-year-old daughter, just happened to see we were walking by the Black Mariah, the Alcatraz paddy wagon. That was all we were doing—*walking by it*. But when Darby saw the Mariah had a flat tire, who do you think got the blame?

Yours truly.

It couldn't have been Darby drove over a nail. Oh no. It had to have been us. We had to go with him to San Francisco and carry a new tire down Van Ness Avenue, to the ferry and up the switchback, to where the Mariah was parked up top. Darby wouldn't even let us roll it on the road. Didn't want it to get dirty. It's a tire! Where does he think it usually goes?

My father wouldn't help us with Darby either. "I know you

had nothing to do with that flat tire, but it won't hurt you to give Darby a hand, Moose," is what he said.

When I first moved here, I thought all the bad guys were on one side of the bars and all the good guys were on the other. But lately, I've begun to wonder if there isn't at least one officer on the free side who ought to be locked up and maybe a convict who isn't half as bad as he's cracked up to be. I'm thinking about Al Capone—the most notorious gangster in America. The worst guy we have up top. How could it be that he did me a good turn?

It doesn't make sense, does it? But Al Capone got my sister, Natalie, into a school called the Esther P. Marinoff where she'd been turned down twice already. It's a boarding school for kids who have their wires crossed up. It's a school and not a school . . . a place to make her normal.

I don't know for certain it was Capone who helped us. I mean the guy is locked up in a five-by-nine-foot cell. He's not allowed to make a phone call or write a letter that isn't censored word for word. It doesn't seem possible he could have done anything to help us, even if he wanted to.

But out of desperation, I sent a letter asking Capone for help and Natalie got accepted. Then I got a note in the pocket of my newly laundered shirt: *Done,* it said.

I haven't told anyone about this. It's something I try not to think about, but today, the day Nat's finally leaving for school, I can't keep my mind from going over the details again and again.

The thing that stumps me is *why*. I never even met Al Capone . . . why would he help me?

■ ■ ■

I watch Nat as she sits on the living room floor going through our books one by one. She looks almost like a regular sixteen-year-old this morning, if her mouth wasn't twitching right and right and right again and her shoulders were just down where they're supposed to be. She opens a book, fans her face with the pages, then sets the book back on the shelf, just exactly as it was. She has been through one entire shelf this way. Now she's working on the second.

Normally, my mom wouldn't let her do this, but today she doesn't want to take the chance of upsetting her.

"You ready to go, Natalie?" my mother asks.

Nat moves faster. She fans the pages so quickly each book sounds like one quick *ffffrrrt*. All I hear is *ffffrrrt ffffrrrt ffffrrrt* as I look out our front window down to the dock. Sure enough there's Officer Trixle. He's supposed to be off today, but Trixle can't keep his nose out of our business. He's almost as much trouble as Piper, the warden's daughter—only not half as pretty. When you look like Piper does, people forgive a whole lot of things, but never mind about that. What I think about Piper is kind of embarrassing, to tell you the truth.

My father comes out of the bathroom. The toilet is running again. The plumbing in 64 building is held together with bubble gum and last year's oatmeal stuck hard and solid. But luckily for us, Seven Fingers, our very own felon plumber, fixes it for free. Not exactly for free actually. We pay him a chocolate bar every time, but no one is supposed to know that.

"Time to go, Natalie," my mom says.

Natalie is wearing a new yellow dress today. My mother cut the pattern, but the convicts in the tailor shop sewed it. The cons did a pretty good job. Only the belt is bugging Nat. She pulls at it, weaving it in and out of the loops. In and out. In and out. Nat's mouth puckers to one side. "Moose school. Natalie home," she says.

"Not today," my mother says brightly. "Today is your big day. Today *you're* going to school."

"*Not* today," Nat tells her. "*Not* today. *Not* today."

I can't help smiling at this. Natalie likes to repeat what you say and here she's repeating my mom's exact words with a change of inflection that makes them say what Natalie wants them to say and not at all what my mother meant. I love when Natalie outsmarts Mom this way. Sometimes Nat is smarter than we are. Other times, she doesn't understand the first thing about anything. That's the trouble with Natalie—you never know which way she'll go.

The first time Nat went to the Esther P. Marinoff School she pitched a fit the size of Oklahoma and they kicked her out, but I don't think that will happen this time. She's getting better in her own weird way. I used to say Nat's like a human adding machine without the human part, but now she's touching down human more days than not. And each time she does it feels as if the sun has come out after sixty straight days of rain.

"Tell her, Moose. Tell her how wonderful it's going to be," my mother says.

"Tell her, Moose. Tell her how wonderful it's going to be," Nat repeats, picking up her button box and holding it tight against her chest.

"You get to take your buttons, Nat. *Mom* said," I say.

I almost think I see her smile then—as much of a smile as you ever get from Natalie anyway. She peeks inside her button box, checking to make sure all of her precious buttons are exactly where they're supposed to be.

When we head down to the dock, my mom's step is light on the stairs. She's so sure that the Esther P. Marinoff will be the thing that fixes Natalie. My dad's feet are moving to the beat of an Irish jig. Natalie is taking each step carefully and methodically as if she wants each foot to make a lasting impression on the stairs.

When we get down to the water's edge I see Trixle walking across the dock, bull horn in hand.

"*Two hundred yards back please! All boats must stay two hundred yards off the shore!*" Officer Trixle booms through his bullhorn to a tour boat that has come too close to the island.

"Warned him before, that one. Mac'll put a bead on him. Fix 'em good," Trixle tells my father.

Natalie hates loud noises. Once they shot a warning blast into the water when we were in our apartment and she curled up in a ball in the middle of the living room and wouldn't get up for the better part of the afternoon. Another time she didn't seem to hear a gun go off ten feet away. It's impossible to predict what Natalie will do.

"Darby, hey Darby . . ." my father wheedles. "Please—not today, okay, buddy?"

"Got to learn to straighten up and fly right," Darby mutters, "if she's coming back, that is." His eyes are bright with the unasked question.

Before the tower guard can get the boat in his gun sights, it turns starboard and hightails back to the city, and the tick in my mom's cheek relaxes.

Officer Trixle gets a happy little bounce to his step. He motions to the guard tower anyway, and the guard tower officer pelts the bay with a showy spray of firepower that pounds like fireworks exploding inside your head.

Natalie shrieks high and piercing like the escape siren. She closes her eyes, wraps her arms around her head, and begins to rock.

The bullets don't get anywhere near the tour boat, but it roars forward, sinking low behind as it struggles to gain speed.

"Natalie, it's all done now. It's all over. No more guns, okay? No more," I tell her as my mother digs in her bag for the emergency lemon cake.

"They were leaving already," my mom whispers to my father. "That was completely unnecessary."

"He's just doing his job, Helen," my father says, but his face is pinched like his belt is a notch too tight.

Nat's arms stay wrapped around her head like a bandage. She rocks from foot to foot, still making her little shrieks.

Trixle hitches up his trousers and walks toward us. He stares at Natalie. "Got a problem here, Cam?"

"No problem. We got it under control," my father's voice is confident and commanding like a Boy Scout leader's.

Trixle sucks on his lip. "Don't look that way to me."

"Just scared her is all," my father tells him.

Trixle clears his throat. "Gonna have to do an incident report on this, Cam. Warden's orders."

My father frowns and lowers his voice as if he's letting Trixle in on a secret. "Nothing to worry about here, Darby."

Darby makes a juicy noise with his spit. "Anything out of the ordinary, I got to report."

My mom picks up Nat's suitcase, hoping to distract her and get her away from Darby. "Let's go, Nat," she says.

"But what about Jimmy and Theresa?" I ask. "They wanted to say goodbye. Couldn't you wait? I can run get them. It will only take a minute." Theresa is Jimmy's little sister and she's really good with Natalie.

My mom shakes her head. Nat's shrieking has subsided. Now it's more like the hum of a radio gone haywire. But my mom clearly wants to get her out of here.

I don't think Nat will go, but she does. She's still humming, still holding her head, but she's walking along behind my mother, yes she is.

"Bye Nat." I wave stiffly.

"Moose bye. Moose bye," she says as she toe-walks across the gangplank.

I take a step forward. I know better than to try to hug her. Nat hates to be touched, but I want to go get the Mattamans at least. I promised I'd let them know when she was leaving.

My father puts his hand on my arm. "She can't take much more hullabaloo," he murmurs, his eyes on Darby Trixle, who is deep in conversation with the buck sergeant.

My mom waves to us from the starboard side, scooting Nat's suitcase under the seat. Nat sits down, her eyes trained on her lap. The motor roars to a start and the *Frank M. Coxe* pulls out fast, carving a white wake in the stirred-up brown water.

We watch until the boat is so small it could fit in the finger of my baseball glove. And then it's gone.

2. THE SECRET PASSAGEWAY

■ ■

Same day—Monday, August 5, 1935

There's nothing like baseball to get your mind off of things you'd rather not think about. The smell of the glove, the feel of the ball, that *thwack* the bat makes when you hit one out of the park. . . . It's enough to cure anything bad that could ever happen. And today is a baseball day, because my friend Scout from school is coming to Alcatraz this afternoon. Scout is Mr. Baseball. He has his own team and he can really play.

I tell Jimmy all about this inside the crawlspace under 64 building that runs beneath apartment 1D, a vacant apartment, to 1E, Mrs. Caconi's place. The crawlspace is in what we like to call Chinatown because it looks like the alleyways in Chinatown in San Francisco. Normally, the crawlspace is locked, but last week Jimmy saw the screws in the door hinge were loose, so he took off the hinge and we opened the door. When we leave, we put the hinges back and the door seals up tight like no one has ever been inside.

The only problem is it's dark in here—everything is coated with an inch of dust and you have to crawl on your hands and knees, avoid the ant holes, and watch the beams so you won't clonk your head. The cobwebs alone could kill you the way they descend like gauze over your mouth and you breathe 'em in and hope you haven't sucked a spider down your throat. Still, it's a good place to talk things over. In our secret passageway, we say things we wouldn't say anywhere else. I like that no one knows about this place except Jimmy and me.

I can't imagine a better spot than underneath Mrs. Caconi's apartment either. The moms on the island spend a lot of time at Mrs. Caconi's the way the kids gravitate toward the parade grounds. I think it's because Mrs. Caconi doesn't have kids, so they get a break from us at her place—kind of like the teachers' lounge at school.

Our best day last week we heard Mrs. Caconi and Officer Trixle's wife, Bea, discussing hair that grows out of your ear hole. Apparently Darby Trixle has big bushes of ear hair Bea has to clip every week. We could hardly keep from laughing out loud when we heard this.

That's the one thing we have to be wary of down here: noise. We're pretty sure they can hear us in the apartments above, if we aren't really quiet.

"Hey Jimmy, you working today?" I ask once we determine no one is in Mrs. Caconi's apartment.

Jimmy's been helping Bea Trixle, who runs the canteen, our island store. He doesn't get paid for it, but whenever he works, Bea gives his mom a discount on whatever she buys. Sometimes Theresa helps too, but only if Janet Trixle isn't around. Theresa is the same age as Janet, but she and Janet can't stand each other. According to Theresa, Janet's only real interests are rules and collecting stuff for her fairy jail.

"I'm off at two," Jimmy says. "You gonna bring Scout to see the flies?"

Jimmy really likes flies. He knows a lot of unusual facts about them too. Flies puke when they land. Flies taste with their feet. Apparently they puke, then they lick the vomit up with their toes.

"Sure," I say. "But Scout's gonna want to play ball."

In the last few weeks, Jimmy has become my best friend on Alcatraz, despite the fact that he stinks at baseball. If a baseball flew into Jimmy's glove he wouldn't know what to do with it. He'd probably use it to brush his teeth. Maybe he'd plant it in the ground to grow a big old baseball tree. The kid has no idea.

Jimmy's nose lifts in the air—*ah, ah, ah choo*. He sprays me with snot and knocks his glasses off.

I wipe off my arm. "Thanks a lot, Jimmy," I say.

Ah, ah, ah choo. He sneezes again, but this time he turns his head away and gives the ants a bath instead of me. "You want me to play?" he asks.

"Of course," I say. "I always want you to play."

Jim cocks his head as if he doesn't quite believe this. "But Scout plays all the time. He's good, right?"

"He's not great or anything."

Jimmy grins. "Oh, okay. Me neither."

I don't know what to say to this. Even in our secret place it seems better not to tell Jimmy that Scout's "not great" is so much better than Jimmy's "not great" that it isn't fair to compare the two.

"C'mon, let's go. I want to find Annie and get my arm warmed up before Scout gets here," I say.

Crawling back Jimmy picks his way slowly and carefully,

stopping every time he has a question. "Think Scout'll like my fly project?"

Jimmy's latest project is to teach flies tricks. He wants to hold a circus and charge admission.

"Course," I say.

Jimmy starts moving forward, then he stops again. "Think Scout will like me?"

"Sure. I told him all about you."

Jimmy considers this. "Good, because I've got a new idea. I'm thinking the problem is quantity. I don't have enough flies."

I sit back on my haunches and wait while Jimmy launches into a technical explanation of his breeding plans. There is no stopping Jimmy Mattaman when he gets talking about his flies.

When he finally gets to the door, I scamper after him, covering the same ground in one-third the time. "You're fast," he observes.

"You're slow," I tell him as we press our ears against the frame to listen for unusual sounds, but it's all quiet. We crack open the door a few inches; still nothing. We push it the rest of the way and Jimmy—because he's smaller—pokes his head out.

"All clear," he whispers, and we jump down.

Just as Jimmy finishes replacing the screws in the hinge, we hear footsteps on the old cement stairwell. "Uh-oh," I whisper as I spot shiny black guard shoes coming down.

"Thought you was working this morning, Jimmy?" Darby bellows through his ever present bullhorn.

"Yes, sir," Jimmy says.

Darby peers over the railing, but he can't see me because I'm getting the baseball gear I stashed in one of the storage rooms. "What you doing down there?" he asks Jimmy.

"Nothing, sir," Jimmy answers.

"Nothing, huh? Do I look like I was born yesterday, Jimmy?" Darby asks.

"No sir," Jimmy replies, skedaddling up the stairs. Jimmy doesn't say anything about me. He knows it's better if Darby doesn't see me. Darby hates me on account of I'm Natalie's brother. Natalie really bugs him.

I stand quietly, waiting for them to leave. When they're gone, I climb up to apartment 3H, Annie Bomini's place. Annie's the only kid on the whole island who's any good at baseball. What a shame she's a girl.

I peer through the screen door, focusing on the wooden table in the Bominis' living room. It was made by the cons in the furniture shop that Annie's father runs. The Bominis have a lot of wood stuff plus needlepoint everywhere. Needlepoint pillows, tablecloths, tissue holders, seat covers. Mrs. Bomini has a needlepoint toilet cover for every day of the week. I don't know why you need a *Monday* toilet seat cover on Mondays. Is it that important to know what day it is when you do your business?

"Annie, c'mon," I call, hoping Mrs. Bomini isn't around. Mrs. Bomini is a one-woman talking machine. Once she gets you cornered you pretty much have to have a heart attack and be carried away on a stretcher before she'll stop.

Annie's skin is pale, and her hair is so blond it's almost

white. She looks twelve but kind of old too, like forty-two. She's squarish from head to foot, like God used a T-square to assemble her.

Annie props open the screen door with her foot. "Moose." She gulps, her big flat face looking pinched today. "You won't believe what happened."

Uh-oh, what if she doesn't want to play? That's the trouble with girls. They have to actually *feel* like playing.

"What happened?" I ask.

"We got the wrong laundry. We got yours," she whispers.

Laundry . . . that is the one word I don't feel like hearing right now. Ever since I got that note from Al Capone, I've been very careful to be the first person to get my laundry in case he decides to send another note. My mom has even noticed. "Why, you're taking care of your own laundry now Moose, isn't that nice," my mom said.

"So? Just give it back." I try to keep my voice from sounding as panicky as I feel.

"I didn't realize it was your laundry. I started putting it away and . . . Moose, there was a note in the pocket of your shirt."

"A-a note?" My voice breaks high like a girl's.

My hands shake as she gives me a scrap of paper folded twice. My mind floods with things I don't want to think about. Al Capone, the warden's office, Natalie being thrown out of school.

The note is written on the same paper in the same handwriting as the other one. *Your turn*, it says.

My face feels hot and sweaty, then cold and clammy. I check the back and then the front again for any other words and stuff the note in my pocket.

Annie's blue eyes bulge. "Your turn? What's it your turn *for*, Moose?"

"I dunno," I mutter, my mind scrambling to make sense of this.

Her eyes won't let go of me. She seems to sense there's more to this than I'm saying. "Who is it from?" she asks, her face pained like she just swallowed a jawbreaker.

I hunker down away from her. "It must be a mistake," I say, but my voice feels distant, like the words are coming out of a cave in my chest.

"A mistake?" she asks. "That's what Darby Trixle said when the laundry cons sewed his fly shut."

"That wasn't a mistake, but *this* is," I say louder than I mean to. "Just like you getting our laundry was a mistake." I'm proud of myself for making this connection. It sounds so reasonable.

Annie bites her lip. She's watching me.

"Did you tell anyone?" I ask her.

"Haven't had time to tell anyone. It just happened."

I breathe out a big burst of relief. "Are you *going* to tell anyone?"

"Depends." She squints at me. "Are you gonna level with me?"

"Look, I don't know that much about this," I say, but my words sound flimsy, like they need a paperweight to keep from floating away.

Annie is looking at me intently. "I thought we were best friends."

I stare back at her relentless blue eyes. "We are best friends."

Annie is tough. She won't let up.

I bite my lip. "You better swear swear, double swear, hope to die if you lie."

"C'mon, Moose. You know I keep my word. I always do."

She's right. She always does. But this is something else again. It's not like keeping quiet about when we saw Associate Warden Chudley relieve himself in Bea Trixle's pickle barrel. This could get me kicked off the island. But if I don't explain what's happening, she'll tell for sure. I don't have much choice here.

"I asked Capone for help to get Natalie into the Esther P. Marinoff School and then she got in and he sent me a note that said Done." I can't get the words out fast enough.

"You *what?*" she snaps, her chin jutting out with the shock of what I've just told her.

I explain again, slower this time.

"And then what happened? After the note?" Annie demands.

"Nothing happened after the note."

"So Natalie went to school today because Capone got her in and you never told anyone and then you get this *Your turn* note. *That's* the truth? You swear it?"

"It's the truth, except somebody else knows a little. Piper. She knows I sent Capone a letter. When Nat got in, she asked me about it but I told her it was because the Esther P. Marinoff opened a school for older kids. That's what they told my parents. That's the reason they think she got in too."

That's not the only thing Piper knows that I wish she didn't. She also knows that my sister made friends with convict #105. Having your sister, who isn't right in the head, befriend a grown man convicted of a terrible crime isn't my idea of fun. In fact, I'd rather run buck-naked down California Street than have that happen again. But that's a whole other story I hope never to tell. Alcatraz 105, aka Onion, got sent to Terminal Island and then released, so he's not on Alcatraz anymore. I don't have to worry about him ever again.

"But no one knows about Capone's notes?"

"Nope."

"You know what he wants, don't you?" Annie whispers. "Payback."

"But how would he even know Natalie left today?" I ask weakly.

She frowns. "Cons know everything that happens on this island, you know that."

"Yeah, but why didn't he say what he wanted? If it had been me, I would have asked for double chocolate brownies with no nuts, the sports page, the funny papers, vanilla sucking candy, French fries, a cheeseburger, a book on the Babe. He didn't ask for *anything*, Annie."

"He wants to make you sweat," Annie says. "He's the cat and you're the mouse. Back home in Omaha we had a barn cat who would get a mouse, play with it for a few hours, then take it off to a dark corner and eat the head off."

"So nice of you to put it that way," I growl.

Annie nods, ignoring my sarcasm. "It's true and you know it. You sure this is only the second note?"

"Of course I'm sure," I snap at her.

Her blue eyes have gone watchful now. "This is serious, Moose."

"*You think I don't know that?*"

"So what are you going to do? I mean if anyone found out

you did a favor for Capone, your dad would be fired"—she snaps her fingers—"like that."

"Any more good news for me?"

"And you know what else? If Capone got Natalie into the Esther P. Marinoff, he could get her kicked out too." She crosses her arms. "You're cooked either way, Moose."

"Thanks, Annie, that makes me feel great," I whisper.

Annie shrugs. "Well it's true."

"Look, Annie. This is good news." I try to make my voice sound as if I believe what I'm saying. "Because really he didn't ask for anything."

She shakes her head. "Don't be a fool, Moose. You should have told before. We have to tell now. No ifs, ands, or buts about it."

"You just said yourself if he got her in, he could get her kicked out." I'm practically shouting. "It's Nat's life we're talking about. This school is her chance."

"You're crazy if you help Al Capone!"

"I'm not helping him."

She sighs, bites her bottom lip. "I shouldn't have promised not to say anything."

"Yeah, but you did promise."

She bugs her eyes out at me. "I know, okay?"

"Look, this isn't about you. Can't you just pretend you didn't find the note?" I'm pleading with her now.

"I'm not good at pretending."

"You swore, Annie!"

"I know!" Annie growls.

I feel the stitches on the baseball in my hand, and I think back to last year when we lived in Santa Monica and my gram helped us with Natalie. Things were better back then. It's too hard here with just my mom, my dad . . . and me.

"So are we going to play ball?" I whisper.

Annie rolls her eyes. "Jeepers, Moose. Something like this happens and all you can think about is baseball?"

"Yeah," I say. "It is."

3. WILLY ONE ARM

Alcatraz Island is shaped like a wedding cake with three tiers and lots of paths and stairs and switchbacks that lead from one tier to the next. The parade grounds where we play baseball is a big, flat parking lot–size cement area in the middle tier of the island. It makes a pretty good field except for the wind. I can't tell you how irritating it is to hit a good ball and have the wind make it a foul.

Annie and I are playing catch right now, which gets my mind off of Capone, but it doesn't seem to distract Annie one bit. Every other throw she's walking up to whisper another suggestion. I should wash my own laundry, so Capone won't have a way to communicate with me. I should talk to the people at the Esther P. Marinoff School. I should come with her to church. The priest will know what to do.

"I'm not even Catholic," I tell Annie as Piper flies down the steep switchback on her roller skates, her long hair streaming behind her, her dress flowing back so you can see the outline of her—okay, never mind what you can see. She goes so fast sparks fly from her skates. She shoots up in the air over a crack in the road and lands with a graceful *clickety-clack-clack*.

We're not supposed to race down the switchback, but most

of the grown-ups look the other way when it's the warden's daughter who's breaking the rules. No one ever races Piper, because she always wins . . . either fair and square or the other way. My mom says Piper is twelve going on eighteen and not a good eighteen either.

When Piper stops, she gives us her full movie star smile. "Hi." She runs her hands through her hair and whispers to Annie.

We throw the ball a few times. Me whipping it hard, Annie gutlessly tossing it. She's too upset to concentrate on what she's doing.

The count bell rings like it does every hour on the hour to count the cons and make sure none have escaped. No one pays any attention. It's like the gulls always carping and complaining and the deep rumble of the fog horn. These are the sounds of Alcatraz—the ticking of our own island clock, I guess you could say.

"Hey . . . what's going on with you two?" Piper asks, looking at me, then Annie, then me. "You aren't insulting each other."

"Nothing," Annie and I answer in unison.

Piper looks back and forth between us again. "No, really."

"Nothing is going on," Annie says, louder this time.

Piper laughs. "Annie, you're such a bad liar," she says.

Piper is right. Annie is a terrible liar. It's only been five minutes and Piper already knows something's up. Of course, I'm not much better.

"Well stop it." Piper shakes her finger at us. "Just, you know, kiss and make up."

Annie snorts. "I'm *not* kissing him." She throws the ball hard for once, her cheeks flushed. "That's your job, Piper."

"Are you kidding, I wouldn't kiss Moose if you paid me a hundred dollars, a thousand dollars, a million . . . " Piper says as she skates by me.

"Sure you wouldn't," Annie mutters, throwing the ball so hard it practically blisters my hand.

"I wouldn't," Piper insists. "Can you imagine kissing Moose? It would be like kissing a . . . a . . . bagpipe."

"A bagpipe?" I say. "Thanks a lot."

"Hey Moose, did you know Piper's got cons working in her house?" Annie asks.

"Right, Annie," I say, rolling my eyes.

"Actually, I do." Piper smiles brightly like her daddy just bought her a new puppy. "Buddy Boy is a confidence man—you know, a con artist—he's our houseboy, and Willy One Arm is a thief. He's our cook."

I stretch up to catch Annie's fly ball, stop it with my glove, then turn and face Piper full on. "What are you, crazy?"

"Her mom needs extra help. She's in a family way," Annie explains.

"Did you have to bring that up?" Piper snaps.

"It's not a secret. One look at her and you can tell. Besides your father has been telling everybody in the universe."

"You don't know the half of it so just shut up okay, Annie?" Piper growls.

"Wait . . . Piper's mom needs extra help *from a thief?*" I ask.

"He's not going to steal anything." Piper snorts. "Being a passman is the best convict job on the whole island. Why would he risk losing a job like that?"

I shake my head. "Why would you break the law and get yourself locked up for life? You think these guys are logical?"

Piper puffs up her chest. "Cons won't mess with the warden. They wouldn't dare."

"So what then . . . your mom's going to hand her baby over to a one-armed felon? Hands up." I pretend to aim a pistol. "I have a loaded diaper right here."

Piper laughs. I like the sound of her laugh. I can't help it, I do.

"Rock-a-bye baby, in the cell house up top," I sing. "When the wind blows the cradle will rock. When the cons make a break, the cradle will fall, and down will come baby, handcuffs and all."

I pretend to carry a tray with one hand, the other arm tucked behind my back. "Where's Willy One Arm's other arm? Think about that after he serves you your supper."

Now Piper is doubled over laughing.

I strum an imaginary guitar and sing, "Where, oh where, do the stray arms go? Where oh where—"

"Moose, stop it, okay? We have to talk," Annie barks.

"Uh-oh. She's serious." Piper mimics Annie, waggling her head.

Annie glares at Piper, then her eyes find me.

"Oh by all means talk, then," Piper says, her voice heavy with sarcasm.

"We don't need to talk," I tell Annie.

Annie glowers at me. "Yes, we do."

Piper's laugh turns raspy again. "You guys sound like Bea and Darby Trixle when Darby forgot their anniversary. Remember how she locked him out of the apartment and he had to stay in the bachelors' quarters?"

Annie and I stare at each other, ignoring Piper.

Piper shrugs her shoulders. "Okay, fine, don't tell me what's going on, I don't even care." She pauses as if she's waiting for us to fill her in.

Annie and I continue to stare at each other, like we're in a competition and we lose points if we blink.

Piper flicks at the cement with her skate. "You want to have secrets, go right ahead," she says as a bullhorn booms across the parade grounds.

"*Moose Flanagan!*"

Uh-oh . . . not Trixle again. He's got Janet with him too. She's carrying her own bullhorn—a small one, but it works. There's no separating either of them from their bullhorns. They probably use them at the dinner table. "*PLEASE PASS THE POTATOES!*"

I grasp the ball in my glove and run across the parade grounds. "Yes, sir," I say. Janet has her hair braided so tightly it gives me a headache to look at her. She stands behind her father, holding the bullhorn at the ready. Theresa says whenever they play together and Janet doesn't like something, she bellows into her bullhorn and her parents come running.

"You have a friend visiting today?" Darby asks.

"Yes, sir."

"His name?"

"Scout McIlvey."

Trixle takes out his handkerchief and blows his nose. His jacket is too small. It pulls across his back, making his muscles bulge and his shoulders pinch together. He puts his handkerchief back in his pocket and looks down at his clipboard. "Supposed to be on the one o'clock boat. You understand that you must get a signed permission for the exact boat a visitor is on?"

"Yes, sir."

"And you must meet the boat your visitor is taking?"

"Yes, sir."

"And keep your visitor with you at all times?"

"Yes, sir."

"I'm not sure who let him on—"

"What do you mean, sir, who let him on? He's here now?" I ask.

"Not now. No. Without the correct paperwork, I had to send him on his way."

"You sent him *away*?"

Janet can't cover her smile now. It's popping off her face. She lives for stuff like this.

"He's not supposed to be on the ten o'clock. What did I just explain to you?"

"Mr. Trixle, please . . . Scout was here and now he's gone?"

He nods his pin head. "Without the correct John Hancock I had no choice but to—"

I'm practically flying down the switchback, my feet barely making contact with the road. But I don't need to get too far before I see the *Coxe*, our ferry, on its way back to San Francisco.

The boat was in the dock for twenty whole minutes before it headed out again. Trixle had waited until they weighed anchor to come find me. Of course he did.

4. MURDERERS AND MADMEN

▪ ▪

Same day—Monday, August 5, 1935

I head for San Francisco on the next boat, but Scout isn't waiting for me at Fort Mason. I'll bet Trixle didn't bother to tell him there'd been a mix-up on the time. I'll bet he just said Scout didn't have permission to visit.

Scout doesn't have a phone, so I have to walk all the way to his house in the Marina. When I find him, he takes out the letter I wrote him with the ferry time on it. In between the one and the colon is a blotch of ink that kind of looks like a zero. He thought it was 10:00 instead of 1:00.

Luckily, Scout can still come. In fact, he's so excited about getting to see Alcatraz we practically run the whole way to the ferry, but that's not unusual for Scout. Everything he does is fast. Just being around him I move faster too.

When we get to the island, we head straight for Annie's apartment and rap our bats on her door. I've told Annie all about Scout and I know she's dying to play with him. Scout is humming "Take Me Out to the Ball Game" when the door squeaks open. "Annie, Scout's here. C'mon, let's go." I rotate my hand in quick circles.

But Annie's broad face is set hard. "Can't," she says.

"Why not?"

"You know why not," she whispers, motioning for me to come in.

"No, I don't."

"Yes, you do." She glowers at me.

I groan. "Scout, just a minute, okay?"

Scout nods his fast nod, and I slip inside Annie's apartment and gently shut the door. "What?"

She wraps one arm around the other like she's holding herself in. I wish Annie wouldn't do this. It's what Nat does when she's upset, too, and I don't want to think about Natalie right now. "I can't play with you until you tell," Annie announces.

"About the note?"

Annie rolls her eyes. "What do you think, Moose? Of course about the note."

"For the one hundredth time, Annie, I can't do that."

Annie's arms tighten around herself. "Then I won't play."

"What do you mean you won't play?"

She frowns and shrugs her shoulders, just a little, as if the movement pains her.

"But Annie," I whisper. "Don't you see? I can't wreck everything for Natalie. She's my sister."

Annie shakes her head. "Capone's a gangster. A mob boss. He could kill you. You want to get shot? Jeez, Moose, do I have to explain everything to you?"

"First off, he can't shoot me. He's locked up. And in the second place—"

"He doesn't do it himself, idiot. He has one of his gorillas do it for him."

"And in the second place," I steamroller on, "it's a little late now. I already asked for his help. He already gave it."

"It's not too late. You could explain it all. You could explain everything."

"To the warden?" I snort. "Look Annie, Capone didn't ask for anything."

"He will, though. You know he will."

"And I won't do it."

"Yeah, and then what?"

It feels suddenly hot and stuffy in her apartment. "Look, Annie, this isn't your problem, okay?"

Annie's blue eyes are extra round, like the pressure inside her head is pushing them out of her skull. "I thought you were like me. I thought you didn't like to get in trouble either."

"I am like you. But this is my family, okay? I'm not going to mess this up for Natalie. You wouldn't either, if you were me." I hadn't really decided what I was going to do about all of this, but suddenly this much is clear.

Annie shakes her big square head. "My mom says a school can't make Natalie normal anyway. My mom says everybody knows that . . . except you."

"Annie, shut up, okay? Just shut up!" I squeeze out the door and heave the screen closed. I'm looking for a big slamming noise, but all I get is a flimsy, tinny clap.

Scout squints, looking up at me. I take big, fast steps to get us as far away from Annie as possible.

"She won't play," I mutter as we head for the stairwell.

Scout hops on one foot, takes off his shoe, and dumps out a trickling of sand. "Can't imagine she's any good anyway."

"Oh she's good, all right. She could strike you out."

"Excuse me?" He pokes me in the ribs with his bat. "No girl could strike me out."

Annie shoves open the door behind us. "This girl could," she calls after us.

"Then prove it," Scout shouts back. "Put your glove where your mouth is, sweetheart."

"It's Moose's fault I can't play. Blame *him*," Annie shouts as we round the corner to the stairwell.

Scout snorts. "Dames, they're all the same. Nothing is ever their fault."

Upset as I am, I can't help laughing at this. Scout sounds like somebody's dad when he talks this way.

"Actually"—Scout smiles a little like he's proud of himself for getting me out of my mood—"there are three types of girls in the world: lookers, okey-dokeys, and aunties. Lookers are beautiful. Okey-dokeys are not pretty, but not ugly either, and aunties are . . . they're the other kind. That Annie doll, she's an auntie."

Mad as I am at Annie, I can't let Scout talk this way about her. "Annie's different. She can play ball, I swear she can," I tell him.

"Whatever you say, buddy, but that girl's an auntiey if I ever saw one."

"Nah, she's an okey-dokey," I tell him. Up ahead are the parade grounds. Scout speeds up. I haven't said that's where we play, but he already seems to know.

"Auntie." He drops his bat.

"Okey-dokey." I toss my ball in the air.

Scout catches it with his bare left hand. We throw the ball back and forth, gloveless left to gloveless left.

"Pop flies," I call and Scout throws one up almost as high as the basement on the warden's house, which sits on the top tier of the island. But I catch it, of course I do.

It's impossible to stay upset when you're with Scout.

"How come Annie doesn't go to school with us?" Scout asks.

"She goes to Catholic school—St. Bridgette's."

"Any kid besides Piper live here? *Anybody* who can play? I thought you said there was another kid? Or you know, a stray murderer or something." Scout's eyes light up. "The kind with blood."

"Everybody has blood, Scout."

"On their hands, I mean."

"It's probably been washed off by now. I don't think it's such a good idea to wear blood to court." I raise my hand like I'm pledging. "*I'm not guilty, Your Honor, don't mind this blood or anything.*"

Scout laughs, a little burst that comes out his nose. He throws me a fast ball.

"And besides, the blood will get my ball messy," I call to him.

"And slippery too," Scout shouts back.

Convict baseballs are collector's items on Alcatraz. The convicts play baseball in the rec yard, but the way they play, if they hit the ball over the wall, it's an automatic out, so they're pretty rare.

"Piper got you a convict baseball, remember? What did you do with it?"

"Put it to good use. Can't you get me one?" Scout gives me his aw-shucks look. "I mean if a girl could do it . . ."

I snort. "I actually got you the one Piper gave you. And no, I can't get you another. Maybe we could meet a con though."

"That'll do," Scout agrees.

"It's not trash pickup or laundry day, so we can't run into a con that way," I say.

"Al Capone ever pick up your trash?"

"Nope, never met the guy." I know Scout would be impressed if I told him about the notes from Al, but then he'd tell everyone at school. This I don't need. "There's a thief and a con man who work in Piper's house. Let's go say hello," I say as if I do this every day.

Scout whistles long and low. "A con man, a thief, *and* a looker . . . what are we waiting for?"

"Piper's not a looker," I snap.

Scout grins out of one side of his mouth. "Don't get all worked up now, Moose. I just said she was a looker. I didn't say I was looking, now did I?"

"If you weren't looking, how'd you know she was a looker?"

"Ahh, Moose." Scout sighs. "You're pretty far gone," he declares as we walk up the switchback into the shadow of the cell house, a cement building big as a football field with three floors of prisoners inside. Scout, normally the fastest walker in the world, begins to slow his pace. "That's where they keep 'em?" he whispers, pointing to the looming fortress.

"Yep, that's the cell house."

Scout looks around like he's expecting snipers on the rooftops. "And you just walk out here like this?"

"Unless we run."

Scout doesn't smile. He's all business now. "When I meet the con man and the thief, what do I say? I mean, do I shake hands?"

"Don't shake his stump. I don't think it's polite to shake a stump."

Scout's eyes dart all around as he leans in to whisper, "Do I need a weapon?"

"Uh-huh, they issue machine guns right at the door," I tell him.

"Right, Moose," he says, but even his sarcasm is watered down as we perch on the doorstep of the warden's twenty-two-room mansion, which stands directly opposite the cell house. Even after living here for six months, the cell house still gives me the creeps. It's the bars and the sounds I sometimes hear. Hollers, curse words, and metal cups clanking against the bars. The cons aren't supposed to talk, much less yell, but sometimes all heck breaks loose. That's when it gets scary. Still, when we face Piper's house, it feels like we're on some fancy street in San Francisco.

On Alcatraz, heaven is across from hell.

Scout girds himself up. He stuffs his right hand in his pocket, as if he really does have a weapon in there. He's ready to draw as I press the doorbell, but it's only Piper's pregnant mom who answers.

Mrs. Williams has a round face, eyes the color of worn denim with dark shadows underneath, and the same full lips as Piper. Her pregnant stomach sticks up hard and round like a basketball under her sweater. I try not to look at her belly. It's hard not to think about how it got that way.

"Mrs. Williams, this is my friend Scout McIlvey. He goes to school with us."

"Why, Scout." Mrs. Williams shakes Scout's hand. "What a nice surprise."

A little smile lights up Scout's eyes.

"Piper, honey, come on down, sweetheart," Mrs. Williams calls up the grand staircase. Above her head hangs a spectacular chandelier, with a dozen glistening prisms. A ragtime record spins on the gramophone.

Piper's living room is bigger than our whole apartment. It's twice as long, twice as wide, and twice as tall too.

By the piano a man dressed in khaki pants, a white button-down shirt, and a narrow black tie holds a feather duster. His hair is short, yellow and tightly curled, and he's wearing the kind of tortoiseshell spectacles that college professors and good spellers wear.

"Buddy Boy, this is Scout McIlvey." Mrs. Williams is just as warm with Buddy as she is with Scout. I'm not sure where Piper got her raspy edge, but it doesn't seem to be from Mrs. Williams.

Buddy Boy glides across the carpet and offers his hand to Scout, whose eyes dart in my direction. Scout sucks in a big breath and shakes Buddy Boy's hand with his own trembling one. It's easier to be sure of myself with Scout here getting nervous for me. I stick out my hand and Buddy Boy shakes it hard and slow. His eyes, magnified behind his glasses, are sharp and gray like stones under water. He smiles at me, then smiles again as if he has a whole lot of smiles and he wants to make sure I see every one.

Piper appears at the top of the grand staircase, her hair pulled back in a ponytail with a large green ribbon.

"Scout." Piper half skips down the steps. "What are you doing here?"

"I'm glad we finally get to meet," Buddy Boy says in a low tone. I glance over at him thinking he's talking to Scout, but he's not.

"Yes, sir," I say, hoping Scout doesn't hear this. I don't know if you're supposed to call a convict sir, and I don't want Scout to see me acting dumb around the cons. I'm the one who's supposed to know what I'm doing.

"Come to think of it, I believe I've met your mother, Scout . . . Mabel McIlvey?" Mrs. Williams asks.

"Yes, ma'am." Scout moves near Piper and Mrs. Williams.

"She's in the choir at St. Mark's, isn't she?"

"I've heard lots of good things about you *and your sister*, Moose." Buddy's voice is low, like a cat purring on the wrong note. The sound electrifies the hairs on the back of my neck.

"Thanks, Mr. . . . um . . . Boy." I edge toward Scout and Piper and Mrs. Williams.

"I thought so, yes, a beautiful voice. Clear as a bell. You give her my best, you hear?" Mrs. Williams has a polite smile on her tired face. "All right, you kids. I've got a million things to do this afternoon. You go on into the kitchen, help yourselves to the brownies, and tell Willy I said you could have more than one. He's stingy with those brownies," Mrs. Williams tells Buddy.

"He's superstitious, Mrs. W. Can't have the wrong number of brownies left."

"What nonsense. Talk some sense into him, Buddy, will you?" Mrs. Williams smiles at Buddy, as comfortable with him as if he were her cousin. She walks back into the hall.

Buddy catches my eye. He heads toward the piano with a little jig to his step. He has three toothpicks in his mouth and he's chomping down on all of them.

"Hey, Moose, sweet pea." He turns to wave at me and my invisible sister Natalie with a warm smile.

Natalie isn't here. And how's he know my dad calls her sweet pea anyway? Slowly, it dawns on me, he's doing an imitation of my dad. It's pretty good too.

"My dad, right?" I ask.

Buddy smiles, pleased with himself. He clearly enjoys the spotlight.

"Piper?" I call after her. She and Scout are already on their way to the kitchen. "Did you see that? Buddy did a good imitation of my dad."

"Yeah, I've seen it. He can do everyone. He's *good*."

We both look back at Buddy Boy who has followed Piper's mom to the front door where he is patiently listening to her instructions on cleaning the balustrade. The smile, the toothpicks, the wave, everything that reminded me of my father has vanished. Buddy sees us looking at him. He winks, just the way my dad would wink.

Scout and Piper are walking with their heads close together. "So wait . . . what am I supposed to call him?"

"Willy One Arm."

"I call him Willy One Arm?"

"Well, it's better than Mr. Willy One Arm, isn't it?" Piper is almost through the dining room.

The kitchen is larger than I remember and there's a brand-new electric icebox—the kind that doesn't need ice—and a shiny stove that looks like the pictures in the Sears, Roebuck catalog.

A short wiry man dressed in the same clothes as Buddy Boy stands in the back of the kitchen rolling out dough with his one good arm. The other sleeve hangs down flat and empty.

"Willy One Arm . . . Scout and Moose. Scout and Moose . .

. this is Willy One Arm." Piper introduces us with a proud little smile on her face, like she's showing off a really great baseball card collection.

Willy One Arm waves his one good arm, then shakes his stump, which makes the empty sleeve jiggle in the air, but it's the pocket of his shirt that has my attention. There's something moving inside it. Something alive!

"He does sleeve tricks. Want to see?" Piper asks.

Willy One Arm's shoulder begins to move in a circular motion, pivoting his sleeve around with it. He gets it going pretty fast, before he catches his empty sleeve with his one hand and slows it to a stop.

"Wow," Scout says. "That was good."

My eyes are focused on his pocket. What's he got in there?

Willy One Arm gives a little bow. He takes his good hand and sticks it inside his shirt pocket. When he brings it out, a mouse the size of a half-smoked cigar sits on his finger. The mouse is a smoky brown color with dirty bitten-up ears and a twitchy pink nose. Willy One Arm brings the mouse close to his face, as if he's telling her a secret. "Molly, this here is Moose and Scout," Willy says.

Piper moves her hand toward Molly, but Molly dives back inside Willy One Arm's pocket with only her raw, hairless tail showing. Willy One Arm coaxes her out again and begins scratching her head with one yellowing fingernail. Molly clearly loves this.

"How'd you get a mouse?" I ask.

"Found you in the yard, didn't I?" Willy One Arm's squeaky voice tells the mouse. Willy One Arm lets Molly climb on his shoulder, then he lifts the wax paper off of a plate of brownies and offers us each one.

"Mom said we could have two, Willy."

Willy One Arm's mouth begins to twitch. "Monday ain't a good day for fifteen," he mutters in a raspy, rodentlike squeak. He takes a butter knife and cuts three brownies in half. "There," he says. I watch him with the knife. I can't believe they let convicts have knives. It's only a butter knife, but still.

Scout takes two brownies. He's standing a good distance from Willy One Arm with his nervous foot tapping. As I reach for mine, Willy mutters to Molly, "No nuts for Moose."

I get a chill like something awful is crawling down my back. My voice falters. "How do you know I don't like nuts?"

"Piper told us," Willy One Arm replies.

"You did?" I ask her.

Piper rolls her eyes. "God, Moose. Of course. How else would he know?"

Scout is looking at his brownie like he's dying to take a bite, only he isn't quite sure it's safe. He gives me a sheepish smile.

"That's poison. It's a poison brownie. You better give it to me," I whisper, snatching the brownie right out of his hand.

Scout laughs, grabs it back, and takes a bite.

"He's cute when he eats," Piper declares, her eyes on Scout. "He's cute when he isn't eating too."

"Gee thanks, doll," Scout says, a little grin on his face.

Piper takes a step toward him. "*You* wouldn't keep secrets from me, would you?"

"I don't know any secrets. But if I find out any you'll be the first doll I'll tell." Scout turns to me. "C'mon, let's find that Jimmy guy and play ball."

I can hear Piper laugh as we thunder down the switchback.

"Thanks a lot, Scout," I tell him.

"What?" he asks over the sound of our pounding feet.

"Do you have to be so chummy with her?"

"The girl's got murderers and madmen living in her house. I'm telling her whatever the heck she wants to hear." Scout is panting as we slow down.

"They aren't living there."

"Close enough, Moose, close enough."

5. AUNTIE'S REVENGE

■ ■

Same day—Monday, August 5, 1935

Scout and I head straight for the Mattamans' apartment, which smells warm and cinnamony. Big band music plays on the radio as we walk through the living room to Theresa and Jimmy's room. Jimmy has divided the room in half with a curtain he's made out of bottle caps. He collected a billion of them, then threaded string through holes he punctured in the caps. But even without the dividing line, it's easy to see what is Jimmy's and what is Theresa's. Jimmy's side is loaded up with extra parts from a crystal set he's constructing out of a Quaker oats box, a big pile of paper airplanes all folded together in one neat stack, and a rock-shooting machine he hasn't gotten to work yet. His head is bent over a book about flies.

On her side, Theresa has two life-size paper men shot up with bullet holes from the firing range, newspaper articles about Al Capone, Bonnie and Clyde, and Baby Face Nelson and a collection of cat toys she's knitted just in case the warden changes his mind and says she can get a cat. Theresa is busy writing in her notebook of strange convict occurrences. She keeps a list of stuff she thinks are suspect. She has some odd things on the list too, like a full moon. We can't seem to get her to understand that full moons happen no matter where you live.

Theresa has quite the imagination.

"Hey." Jimmy smiles up at us. "Want to know the best way to breed flies?"

"Sure," Scout says.

"They like garbage, feces, cadavers, and carcasses," Jimmy tells us proudly.

"Cadavers? What are cadavers?" Scout asks.

"Dead bodies," I explain.

Scout looks at me sideways. "Where do you keep the dead people?" he whispers.

"We don't have any." I pull a long face. "There's a morgue, but it's empty. I'm very sorry, Scout."

Scout grins and snaps his fingers. "Darn," he says.

Jimmy doesn't smile. He adjusts his glasses. "We need more flies, because so many don't survive the training," he explains.

"Fly training?" Scout asks, incredulously.

"Uh-huh." Jimmy's eyes get bright, but before he can start explaining, Scout jumps up, full of his usual enthusiasm. "You play ball, right, Jim? C'mon, buddy, let's go."

Jimmy pushes a clump of dark curly hair off his forehead. He looks at me like he's expecting me to throw him a life preserver.

"You want to play, Jim?" I ask.

Scout squinches his lips. "Why wouldn't he want to play?"

Jim ignores this. "Where's Annie?" he asks.

"She's mad," I tell him.

Theresa looks up from her notebook. "Why's Annie mad?" she asks from behind the bottle cap curtain.

Scout nods toward Theresa's side of the room. "Does she play? Because I've taught my sisters pretty good. In a pinch they can play outfield. You know, if there aren't enough fellas."

Theresa's head pops through the bottle caps making them clatter like tiny galloping horses. She waves her arm all around, like she's raising her hand at school. "Can I? What about me?"

Scout parts the curtain to get a better look. "How old are you?"

"Eight."

"She's seven," I tell him.

Theresa juts her chin out. "Almost eight, in a couple of days."

Jimmy rolls his eyes. "A hundred is a couple?"

Scout ignores Jimmy. "You gonna do what we tell you?" he asks.

Theresa's mouth presses into a hard thinking line. "I'll get Annie," she decides.

I'm happy to hear this. If anyone can convince Annie to play, it's Theresa. "Yeah," I say, "you do that."

By the time Jimmy, Scout, and I get to the parade grounds, Annie and Theresa are already there. Annie has her gear too!

"I'm gonna play," she announces.

"Swell!" I practically shout. I have no idea why she changed her mind, but I never question the peculiar logic of girls.

"You're *on the bench*." She snatches my glove out of my hand and pokes me in the chest.

"Me?" She can't mean me.

"Yeah, you! Mr. Okey-dokey," she whispers, her voice scratching like a match against flint.

"What are you . . . out of your mind? Course I'm playing."

Annie stretches her arm across her body to warm up her

arm muscles. "No, you're not, Humpty Dumpty, and that's all there is to it."

"Humpty Dumpty?" Scout's lips shake like he's trying not to laugh. "Is that what she calls you?"

"Nice try. Scout is *my* friend. He came to play with *me*." I tap my glove against my chest.

Scout clears his throat. He'll come to my defense, of course he will. He's not going to play without me. What does Annie think?

"Moose is playing," Scout says.

Really, the gall of that girl, thinking she can kick me out of my own game.

"But maybe you could sit out just, you know, the first few pitches. I gotta see if this girl can strike me out. Moose, you understand," Scout whispers. "Jimmy," he yells. "First base or catcher?"

My mouth is hanging open. I can't believe this.

"First," Annie answers for Jimmy.

"Hey, that's *my* position."

Annie glares at me. "Jimmy does all right." She scowls. "He just needs practice."

"You gotta use me. You don't have enough players without me," I tell Scout.

Annie throws him the ball, and he catches it. Back and forth, back and forth it goes. I might as well be a crack in the cement. I climb on top of a wooden crate we call the bench. It won't be long to wait, I tell myself. Scout will hit and then I'll play.

"We'll play with one base. Theresa, you're batter up," Annie commands.

"No wait. It has to be Scout," I insist.

"Nope, Scout's second. I got to warm up."

"Forget it, Annie. I'm not going to sit here for—"

"She has to warm up her arm, buddy," Scout shouts. "Otherwise she'll say it wasn't fair."

What is this? How long am I going to have to sit here and just watch?

Theresa is batter up. She's facing the wrong way and holding the bat cross-handed. Scout seems to know just how to deal with this. He calls a halt to the play and runs up to her for coaching.

When he's finished, Annie spins one to her. Looks like a strike, but it's a ball.

"Ball one," I shout. I may be on the bench, but I'm sure as heck going to ref.

Annie squints at me like I made a bad call. She winds up and pitches another. This one splits the plate in half and Theresa hits it, which seems practically impossible given she'd back to holding the bat cross-handed. It's a wild mis-hit that flies higgledy-piggledy to Jimmy, who watches it go by as if that's what he's supposed to do.

"Jim," Scout yells, "chase it down!"

Jimmy takes off after it.

If I were there, I probably would have caught it on the fly, but no, I'm benched because of Annie. "Okay, Annie, you've had your fun. My turn," I say as Jimmy rolls the ball back to her.

"What was *that*?" Scout asks Jimmy. "Let's try that again." He tosses the ball to Jimmy who catches it, but throws it back his noodley way.

Scout's mouth hangs open. His face stretches out, then

squinches up. "You throw like a girl, Mattaman—a dead girl." He shakes his head. "Theresa," he yells, "*you* take first base."

"Hey!" Annie shouts. "Who made you coach?"

"Just let me play and we won't have this problem," I call out.

But Scout and Annie ignore me. The two of them are staring each other down, the challenge blistering between them. Jimmy is gone. He's over by 64 building now, watching from an angry distance. Theresa is on first base, a sneaky smile on her lips. It's not often she gets to upstage her brother this way.

"You're in trouble, buster," Annie bellows. "I'm going to strike you out, you betcha."

"In your dreams, doll," Scout yells back.

"I'm not a doll, I'm an auntie, remember?" Annie snaps.

"You weren't supposed to hear that. It's not for delicate ears," Scout tells her.

"Delicate? You think I'm delicate?" Annie's jaw moves like she's grinding her teeth. She shuffles her feet as if she has to have the exact right place to get her pitch just so. "This one is for you, Jimmy!" She waves her glove at Jimmy, now standing by the playground slide that the convicts made for us.

Scout picks up the bat. "I don't think so, dolly. But hey, you give it all you got, gal." Scout chews his gum, smacks it, cracks it, rubs his hands on his pants and wraps them around his bat again.

The next pitch catches a corner of the strike zone.

"Strike," I call.

"I thought you said you could hit anything," Annie bellows.

Scout glares at me like this is my fault. "That was just lucky," he mutters. She pitches again. This time it's solidly in the strike zone, but Scout's timing is off. He swings and misses.

Annie's lips quiver with the effort to keep the smile off her face. Now when she winds up, she's sure of herself. She delivers the pitch. It's good. But Scout's mad. He smacks it hard—so hard it flies over 64 building, bounces on the roof, making a tinny sound, then sails over dockside. It's the best hit I've ever seen from him.

I chase after the ball, which is apparently all I'm good for. But it's my ball, for cripes' sake. Just my luck it will roll into the bay.

Scout runs too. He makes it to base and back again, while I clatter down the 64 building steps to the dock. I see my ball over by the patch of garden the cons just planted, but it's still rolling, picking up speed. My eyes are glued to the ball, which seems to be trying to decide which way to go as I thunder after it. I'm just getting close when I notice Seven Fingers and Trixle. Seven Fingers has a shaved bald head. He's lean but strong and tall. Trixle is much shorter, more compact, and bristling with muscle as if everything inside him is combustible.

It's Seven Fingers who snags the ball with his three-fingered hand. I wonder what it feels like to throw a ball with three fingers. He tosses the ball effortlessly. I catch it barehanded.

"You kids aren't supposed to be playin' ball over here," Trixle barks. "You know that."

"We weren't. I mean I'm not. Scout hit a good one. It cleared the building," I explain.

Trixle nods, but his eyes don't believe me. He was born suspicious. "On our way to your place, Moose. You folks got the worst plumbing problems in 64 building, and that's saying a lot."

"Yes, sir, I'm sorry, sir," I mutter.

Seven Fingers laughs at this. "Boy can't help it if his business too big for the crapper."

"Who the H. asked you?" Trixle growls. He turns to me. "Theresa with you?" he asks, glancing up at his apartment—the biggest in all of 64 building.

"Yes, sir," I say.

"How about my Janet?"

"No, sir."

"How come you never invite Janet?"

"Uh, sir? I never invite Theresa either. She just comes."

His eyes narrow as he smacks his chewing tobacco. "Almost time for your buddy to head home."

"No, it's not."

"You talking back to me, boy?"

"No, sir, I'm not, sir. But he's supposed to eat supper with us."

"He's on the three thirty home. That's what I got. Better get your stuff and skedaddle down there."

"He's only been here since one, sir. That's not right."

"I don't make the rules, boy. Just keepin' 'em is all. And his paperwork says three thirty."

"Yes, sir," I grumble through my grinding teeth.

I head back up the 64 building stairs—the fastest way to the parade grounds—Scout has followed me partway down. "Hey," he says, when I catch up to him. "Was that a convict you were talking to? The guy who threw the ball."

"Yep, that's Seven Fingers," I tell him.

"Seven Fingers? What happened to the other three?" Scout

asks as we climb back up to where Annie and Theresa are waiting for us. Jimmy is there too, closer than he was, but still holding himself at a distance.

"That's the mystery," I tell him. "We wonder whenever our toilets are stoppered up."

"Maybe a finger will come floating back up. What did he do?" Scout whispers.

"Ax murderer."

Scout tries to swallow his gasp. "Wait until I tell my dad.

"So hey . . . Wait! Seven Fingers touched it! This is a *convict* baseball now?" Scout's eyes are wide with appreciation.

I shrug. "I guess so."

"Can I have it? Can I?" Scout asks me.

Annie and Theresa are all crowded around. "You can have mine," Scout says. "We could trade."

I don't like the feel of Scout's ball. The stitches are too high. I shrug. "I guess so."

"So you're just going to give him your baseball?" Jimmy mumbles, his eyes focused on the cement.

I'm not sure what to say to this. "He's my friend."

"Your *best* friend," Scout says.

"And what am I?" Jimmy asks.

"You're my best friend too, but look, Jimmy, you live here. You could just get Seven Fingers to throw you a baseball whenever you want," I tell him. "and besides, I thought you had one."

"Where did you get that idea?"

"I dunno."

"That's not a real convict baseball anyway." Jimmy points at the ball. "You're supposed to find it when the cons hit it over the rec yard wall."

"It's close enough." I shrug. "Anyway, Trixle said you have to go, Scout. I'm sorry."

Annie's shoulders move down a notch. Theresa stamps her foot. "I'm gonna go give him a piece of my mind."

"No, you're not," Annie tells her. "You can't get in hot water with Trixle and you know it."

Scout nods. "Trixle . . . he's the muscled-up officer gave me grief this morning? The one with the little girl follows him around?"

"Yep," I tell him.

Scout nods, holding the ball carefully in his glove. He looks over at Annie. "Didn't strike me out, but you did all right."

"For a girl?" she asks.

Scout thinks about this. "For a pitcher," he says.

She smiles a tiny smile, packed solid with joy. She takes a deep breath. "Good enough to play on your team?"

Scout's forehead creases with all the thinking he's doing about this. He gives his gum an extra loud smack. "You bet, doll. You bet."

6. WHAT CAPONE WANTS

■ ■

Monday, August 12, 1935

My mom goes to San Francisco to visit Natalie today, and when she gets home, her step is light and hopeful. "Went well." She takes off her hat. "Natalie acted like she's been going there her whole life. She settled in just fine. Made a friend of the head lady, a tiny woman named Sadie."

My dad puts his arm around my mom's shoulder. Her knees bend as she snuggles into my father. She is taller than he is without her shoes. In her high heels she towers over him. "She's going to be all right, Cam." My mom's voice is husky. She pats her pockets in search of a hanky.

"We've been around the world a few times on this one," my dad murmurs. "But we made it, honey. We did."

My mom smiles. Her knees sag and she collapses onto the couch as if she simply can't take one more step.

"You look beat," my dad tells her. "Why don't you lie down."

My mom nods and goes into their room.

My father picks up his darts. "I don't suppose you'd like to play your old man, would you?"

"You promise to lose?"

"Me?" He pretends innocence. "You're the one who needs

to go easy. I'm not as young as I once was." He lets a dart fly. It hits the bull's-eye from ten feet back.

"Good day today, Moose. Red-letter day. Nothing can go wrong today. Even Seven Fingers got the plumbing working, you see that?" My dad nods toward the bathroom.

"For now anyway," I say.

"Don't know what the problem is with our plumbing. Trixle thinks it's you, you know." My father jabs me in the ribs.

"Me?" I poke my own chest. "How could it be me?"

My father laughs as he organizes the feathers of a rumpled dart.

"Why do you believe everything Darby Trixle says?" I ask.

"Oh Moose, don't tell me you're still mad about that tire?"

"Trixle sent Scout home because he was on the wrong ferry."

My dad's head wags one way then the other as he draws score columns with a pencil. He puts an *M* with antlers for me. "Darby thinks rules are important."

"Okay, I understand that with Scout, *maybe*. But what about Natalie? He knew it would upset her if he had the guard tower shoot."

"Could be," he admits. He aims a dart carefully and methodically, then lets it rip. A bull's-eye. "Guess I'd rather look for the good in people."

"What about the cons? You look for the good in them too?"

My father shrugs. He nods toward the cell house. "Just a bunch of big kids up there. Chuckleheads every one."

"Yeah, but do you believe they're good guys?"

"Nope. And don't you believe it either."

I'm concentrating on the bull's-eye. I feel the dart between my fingers.

"Doesn't mean I don't treat them with respect. Treat a man like a dog, he'll act like a dog. Treat a man with respect, he'll remember that too. But trust them? Not on your life."

"What about the passmen?" I ask let the dart fly. It lands two rings short of a bull's-eye. "The warden has to trust them, right?"

My dad watches me as I move the dart back and forth in the air but don't let go.

"You gonna throw that dart or just play with it?"

"Don't rush me," I say.

I take a deep breath and let it go as the dart zings through the air and lands three rings from the center.

"Not bad." my father nods, looking carefully as if he is contemplating the exact angle of the dart. "I'll tell you the truth here, son, if you keep it between us. Can you do that?" He measures my response with his eyes.

"Course," I tell him, straightening up to my full height.

He takes a dart in each hand. "The warden likes the help—two full-time servants he doesn't have to pay for . . . who wouldn't like that?" He throws first one dart, then the other. "There's no incentive for them to escape on account of they're a few months from release. Plus, he doesn't think they'll fool with him. Him being the warden and all. But I don't buy it. The way I see it, you never get something for nothing." He pulls the darts out, eyeing the line.

"On the other hand, the man knows his business. He ran

San Quentin for ten years. I been at the prison business for what, eight months?" He shrugs. "I'm gonna keep my mouth shut on this one, Moose."

I think about this. "So, I'm supposed to treat the cons with respect but not trust them."

"I don't imagine you kids have much occasion to interact with the convicts. But yes, that's the general idea."

"Okay, Dad, I have another question for you. Have you ever done the wrong thing for the right reason?"

He stops what he's doing and looks over at me. "Why do you ask?"

"Just wondering," I say.

He nods. "You want to play again?"

"You gonna lose this time?"

"Oh definitely." He picks up a dart. "I ever tell you about when I met your mother?" He smiles. "She was going out with my cousin Harold at the time. I took one look at her and I thought, Holy mackerel, there's the girl I'm gonna marry, Harold or no Harold. I'm not proud of that, but I'll tell you what, I sure wouldn't trade your mom for any woman on this planet."

I've heard this story before and it doesn't make me feel any better. I mean, he loved my mom. That's the worst thing he can dredge up from his whole thirty-nine years?

Almost on cue, my mom comes out from her room looking perkier. She gives me a surprisingly radiant smile as she nods to the dartboard. "Let me guess, you got drubbed?"

"Pretends he can't play," I tell her.

"Gotta watch him. He's up to his old tricks again." She gathers up her sheet music.

"You've got a lesson?" I ask.

She blushes. "Thought I might play a bit."

My father and I look at each other. She teaches piano, but she hardly ever plays herself. We don't even have a piano here. She has to walk up to the Officers' Club to play.

"Maybe we could see about getting a piano in here," my father suggests.

"Maybe we could." My mother smiles, her whole face shining like a schoolgirl.

That night when I climb into bed I feel really great for the first time in a long while. My parents are happy. My sister has her chance. I might need to patch things up with Jim, but Scout doesn't come to Alcatraz that often. This isn't going to be a big problem. And Annie will come around. She loves to play ball. She's not going to hold out for long.

My head sinks into my pillow. My chest eases down into the mattress. I'm even getting used to this squeaky old bed and the way the light shines in the doorway. Life is good, I decide as I stick my arm under the pillow to prop my head up. My fingers graze the pillow label. Strange . . . this is the pillow I've always had. I never noticed a label before. I turn over the pillow. A slip of paper with green lines flutters in the air. My heart jams up in my throat, cutting off my air supply.

This can't be another note.

But it is.

Inside the now familiar folds the handwriting looks the same as before:

My Mae loves yellow roses. She'll be on the Sunday 2:00.
Then we're square.

7. ITCHY ALL OVER

■ ■

Tuesday, August 13, 1935

In my dreams Natalie is encased in ice. It's unexplicably hot, hotter than the hottest spot on the equator, hotter than it's ever been before, but the ice won't melt. She is frozen solid in her ice rectangle and nothing I can do will melt it. Annie's big face peers down from the sky. "I told ya so, so, so . . ."

All night I toss and turn. No matter what I do, I can't get comfortable. Every time the sheets touch my skin, I scratch, itch, burn. When I finally get out of bed, I have raised welts in wild irregular shapes all over my body.

"Mommy?"

My mom sticks her head in my room. "Hey there, sleepyhead. It's half past nine already."

"My skin looks funny." I show her the welts all along my belly, my neck, my arms, my back.

She runs her finger over one of them, lightly, carefully. "Hives," she concludes. "You used to get them when you were little."

"What causes them?"

"Could be something you ate. Could be your clothes . . . the detergent."

"The laundry?" my voice squeaks.

"Could be they changed the soap up top."

Suddenly I wonder if this is intentional. What if Al Capone targeted me with itchy soap?

"You ought to take a walk up to Doc Ollie's. See what he has to say about this. Do they itch?"

"Like crazy."

She sits down on my bed and runs her hand over my hair, like I am six instead of twelve. "When you were little, I used to stick you in an oatmeal bath. Did you a world of good. I'll go down to Mrs. Caconi's now, give Ollie a call, see if he has a minute to look at this. You want me to start your breakfast?"

I can't remember the last time my mom made me breakfast. Usually, I just pour my own self some cereal: the cold kind. I'm not going to let this opportunity slide by. "Blueberry pancakes, bacon, hash browns, toast, and some juice and ham too, if you have it," I tell her. "Oh and maybe some scrambled eggs."

She laughs. "That's my Moose. Doesn't let anything get in the way of his appetite. I'll see what I can do."

When she gets back, I hear her banging pans around in the kitchen and then the smell of sizzling bacon.

I hate to admit it, but it's nice having my mother to myself this way. We've been three people and an octopus all of my life, and now the octopus is gone. It's not Natalie that's missing so much as the hubbub around her. The wild-goose chase of what to do and how to help her—one heartbreak chasing another.

What's left now is just my mother and me. How strange this is. How quiet.

But realizing this makes my hives itch all the worse. If I tell my dad what's happening, he'll tell the warden and Natalie could get kicked out of the Esther P. Marinoff School and then the craziness will be back again.

It's up to me to keep her safe.

My blanket is pulled over my head. I breathe in this dark, gray hot itchy space and scratch my skin raw and red.

My mom sticks her head in the door again. "Go on and get dressed, Moose. I want you to get some food in your belly before you go up and see Ollie. He's got time for you at ten."

At the table, she sits with me while I eat, as if she has nothing better to do. "You're a good son, Moose," she says as I help myself to another pancake. "A good brother too. Don't think I haven't noticed."

She averts her eyes when she says this as if she has suddenly revealed too much and embarrassed us both. This is all so peculiar. It's not how my mother usually behaves. She doesn't notice me except as I relate to Natalie.

"You want me to go up to Ollie's with you?" she asks.

This is a ridiculous question. I'm almost thirteen. What if Jimmy or Piper sees me walking up with my mommy. But suddenly my head is nodding yes instead of shaking no.

"You do?" Even she is surprised.

"No, of course not," I mumble, my mouth full of pancakes.

She nods, slowly taking this all in. "I wonder if you'll forgive me," she says in a voice barely audible.

"For what?" I manage to say.

Again her eyes search my face. "For being so wrapped up with Natalie," she whispers.

I stuff my mouth full of more pancake to push the unexpected feelings down.

She picks up my empty milk glass and puts it in the sink, making movements that fill the kitchen with sound. She seems to know I'm not going to answer.

"Go on now. Ollie's expecting you."

Doc Ollie is a stout man with double-thick soled shoes and big deft hands that can thread needles, rock newborns, and gut fish. Doc Ollie can do anything. He's a great whistler to boot, always starts his visits by taking requests.

"'All of Me,'" I tell him today and he whistles two verses.

When I show him my hives, he chuckles. "They certainly do have all of you," he says, making sympathetic clucking noises as he questions me on what I might be allergic to.

"Far as I know, I'm not allergic to anything."

"You doing some worrying?"

I shake my head. "Nope," I say, sucking the inside of my cheek. He is a nice man, Doc Ollie, and I wish I could tell him everything I'm worrying about—give it all to him so it wouldn't be my problem anymore. For a second that almost seems like a good idea. But then I imagine trying to explain to my father how in the world I got our family into this mess.

He nods again. "You nervous about school starting?"

"No, sir."

"Everything okay with your folks?"

"Yes, sir."

"All righty then. I'll get you some salve. Fix you right up. Be all gone few days, but keep it handy because they'll be back. Might take a few weeks 'fore you're good as new."

The salve helps a little, or maybe it's the fresh air. On the way home I start thinking more clearly. Capone must have decided not to send a note in the laundry because of the timing. The boat is coming this Sunday, the laundry doesn't come back until Monday.

It had to have been Seven Fingers who left the note. Trixle is supposed to watch him when he works on the plumbing, but sometimes he and my dad get to talking. What I don't know is why. Why would Seven Fingers leave a note from Capone? Are they friends? Piper once told me every con is either a friend of Capone's or his enemy. People love him or they hate him. That's the kind of man he is.

But the note has made me wonder if Capone is crazy. Does he really expect me to buy a dozen yellow roses and hand them to Mae? If I did that, I would get my family kicked off the island in about thirty seconds. Maybe forty-five. He has to know that, doesn't he?

Why didn't he tell me the name of the hotel where she'll be staying? Then I could have left the roses for her at the front desk. No one would have to know about it. And what did he mean by *Then we're square*? Will I really be off the hook if I do this?

All of this thinking has me back to scratching again. I don't think the salve is working so well now. It's no match for Al Capone.

The thing I keep coming back to is this: If Capone was a regular person and he asked for a couple of lousy flowers to get Natalie in school, I'd think nothing of giving them to him. I'd give a person all the roses in the world for that.

I owe the man. I do.

8. ICEBOX FLY

▪▪▪▪▪▪▪▪▪▪▪▪▪▪▪▪▪▪▪▪▪▪▪▪▪▪▪▪▪▪▪▪▪

Thursday, August 15, 1935

My hives are breeding with each other. They're growing together, merging, enlarging, engorging.

The salve is no help. It may even make them worse. The ones on my ankle are driving me nuts. I've scratched right through my socks. I have them on my neck too, creeping closer to my face.

By the time Mae visits there will be no me left. Just one big hive.

What will happen if I get caught? What will Capone do to me if I refuse? Does he still command his own army of hit men? And if I decide to do this, how will I get the roses? The garden behind the warden's house has flowers, but no roses. I checked. These are the questions that chase around inside my head.

My dad says when you worry too hard, it makes your mind cramp up into a little ball. The best thing is to forget about it. Get some exercise, give your brain a little breathing space.

What I need is baseball . . .and that means Annie.

On the way up to her apartment I plan what to say to convince her to play. But when I get to the Bominis', she isn't even there. "Moose." Mrs. Bomini's blue eyes are round like

Annie's, but in a smaller, older face. She leans out the door and practically sucks me into her apartment. "Come on in. I have two new needlepoint books. I know how you love to see my needlepoint. You're the only boy I know who likes it."

Likes needlepoint? The woman is out of her mind. How am I going to get out of this? Where is Annie?

Mrs. Bomini bears down on me like she's drilling my feet to the floor. Before I know it I am sitting on the sofa with two needlepoint books on my lap and Mrs. Bomini's veiny white hands pointing out one design after another.

She's leaning so close, there's no way to get away. Why does this always happen to me? "Do you think that border is a little too busy?"

"Um, ma'am . . .is Annie around?"

"I sent her down to Bea's to get a few things. But—" She beckons with her finger. "Annie doesn't care for my needlepoint. She's not like you, Moose. Now lookee here, what if I took off some of that blue. Or I could just do this one here?"

"The other one, ma'am, without the border."

"Aren't you a wonder, Moose!" She smiles at me, glowing with pleasure, and turns to another page, where there must be twenty designs marked. This is worse than reading my dad's electrician manuals.

"Now this one, what do you think of this?" She is so close I can smell the tooth powder on her breath. "Such a big flower smack in front like that, I'm concerned it's overpowering. I'm wondering if I might—"

Annie appears suddenly in the door, a bag of groceries in her hand. "Mom!" she barks.

Mrs. Bomini's head drops low on her shoulders. "Now,

Annie . . . Moose likes this, don't you, Moose? " Mrs. Bomini puts her finger to her lips. "It's our little secret, isn't it, Moose?" She giggles.

Annie puts the grocery bag down with a thud. "What's your little secret, Mom?"

"Oh don't you worry." Mrs. Bomini flutters her finger at me. "My lips are sealed about . . . you know."

"Let him get up, Mom." Annie pulls the flour out of the bag, thumps it on the counter.

"Oh for goodness' sake! If a girl can like baseball, surely a boy can like needlepoint."

"Mom, let him up!" Annie barks.

"I have to talk to Annie, ma'am. It's pretty important. Could we finish this later?"

Mrs. Bomini's shoulders sink down, her mouth forms a little pout. "Oh all right," she concedes. "But you bring him back, you hear?" She waggles her finger at Annie.

Annie races around the kitchen unpacking groceries, pouring the flour into the canister, and putting the milk in the icebox. After she's done, she heads outside with me.

"Thanks," I say when we're safely out of earshot of her mom.

She snorts.

"I've been thinking," I tell her. "You know that thing with Capone, you don't need to worry about him. I've worked it out. It's not a problem anymore."

Her eyes move from side to side like she's thinking about this. "Why not?"

"Because. I've taken care of it."

"Which means?" She takes a deep breath and lets it out in

one big burst.

"Because, Annie, please, oh please—" I get down on one knee.

Annie smiles a little at this. "You're cute when you beg," she says.

"Annie, I'll do anything if you'll just play."

"You wanna come back with me?" She bites her lip to keep from laughing. "You know it's okay for a boy to like needlepoint." Annie does a whispered imitation of her mom.

"Anything *except* that."

We both laugh. I think I've got her now, but when we stop laughing she walks the rest of the way up the stairs without another word.

Girls are impossible. Once they decide something, that's it. Guys make deals, make compromises, make things work. Girls just make trouble.

I head down to the canteen to find Jimmy. He's behind the counter, paging through Bea Trixle's receipt book. He sees me and looks down again really quickly.

"Hey, Jimmy," I say.

"Hi, Moose." His voice is cool. He can't still be mad about Scout and the baseball, can he?

Theresa is back in the corner with Baby Rocky on his blanket. Jimmy, Theresa, and the baby of the family, Rocky, all look alike: curly black licorice–colored hair, fair skin, and dark eyes. "We only make one model," Mrs. Mattaman said right after Rocky was born. Theresa has her strange stuff on Alcatraz book out and she's recording things in it.

I wonder where Janet Trixle is. I heard there was a new rule. Theresa is supposed to play with her when she's down here.

It's Janet's mom's canteen, after all. But knowing Theresa, she's figured a way to squirm out of it.

I get a vanilla soda out of the icebox and press my nickel into Jimmy's hand.

He puts it in the cash box, without looking at me.

"Hey, Jimmy." I close my mouth, not sure what to say now. "How are the flies?"

Jimmy's eyes soften. "I got a new idea," he says. "I'm gonna freeze 'em."

"Frozen flies?"

"Then I can get a little leash and collar on them. And it will be like pet flies on a leash."

"Won't it kill them?"

"Jimmy, Rocky has a stinky!" Theresa interrupts, holding her nose. "And it's your turn."

"You bring a diapy?" Jimmy asks. "Like Mom said?"

Theresa shakes her head. "Maybe we could use toilet paper?"

"We can't use toilet paper. Bea will charge us for it," Jimmy tells Theresa. "You figure it out. I'm gonna show Moose the flies."

Theresa sighs. Her face puckers up. "Rocky, oh come on, be quiet, will ya?" She kneels down to give Rocky a toy and pops out the door.

Jimmy opens the icebox and takes out a little box he made out of folded newspaper. It's wet and cold on the bottom. Jimmy bends back a corner of the well-worn lid and I peek in, holding back the damp newspaper with my thumb.

"See, he's still moving around too much. When they get a little colder, they go to sleep and you can slip the thread around their middles," Jimmy explains. He shows me the tiny harness made out of red and yellow braided thread and demonstrates how he plans to slip the harness around the fly. "Trouble is, they die. That's why I need so many.

"Five more minutes," Jimmy decides, latching the icebox with the fly box safely inside as the canteen bell announces a new customer. Jimmy scurries back inside, Theresa right behind him. By the time I get there I see Piper drumming her fingers on the counter.

I take an unexpected gulp of air. I always forget how beautiful she is. Piper plunks her dime down. "Two root beers," she says. "And when's Scout coming back anyway?"

Scout. Does she have to ask about Scout?

Theresa hops behind the counter, takes the dime and inspects it. "Dime's real," she announces, plunking it in the cash register.

"Of course it's real." Piper takes the pop and uncaps it with the opener tied to the counter with a string. She takes a swig. I'm watching her. Staring at her, actually.

"What are you looking at—" Piper starts to say.

"Jiiiimmmmmmmmmmmyyy!" Theresa screams, her voice high and twisted like she's being strangled by invisible hands.

She's standing over Rocky, who isn't crying now. He isn't making a sound. His eyes are panicky and his skin is almost blue. Why isn't he moving?

Jimmy hops the potato bins, knocking over the Cream of Wheat. I'm right behind him, leaping the rolling cylinders of cereal.

"Rooockky! MOOOOOMMMMMMMEEEEEEEE!" Theresa screams.

Jimmy scoops Rocky up in his arms. "Oh jeepers! Doc Ollie! Moose! You're fast. Run him up to Ollie's! TAKE HIM! NOW!" Jimmy's shaking me hard like I've fallen into a stupid sleep.

Piper jams in between us. "Me! Let *me*! *I'm* faster!"

"NO, NOOOOOOOOO!" Theresa pounces on Piper and shoves her against the wall.

Jimmy plunks Rocky in my arms. "Go!" he shouts in my ear. My legs take off.

"I think he swallowed it!" I hear Theresa shout.

The weight of Rocky is warm and heavy against my chest. The screen door slams behind me, ringing the canteen bell.

"MOOOOOMMMMMEEEE!" Theresa is still screaming, but her voice is falling off in the distance.

Out of the corner of my eye I see Jimmy outside Mrs. Caconi's door where the only phone for 64 building is located. *Call Doc Ollie.* The words float through my mind in a blur of my own pounding feet.

Rocky's blanket is flying around my legs. I wind the blanket around my hand as I run, keep running. Don't trip. Don't stop.

"What's the matter? What happened?" somebody yells behind me.

But I'm not stopping. Not answering. I've got Rocky in my arms, I'm not going to look at him, I can't look at him. He's too quiet, too still. I'm afraid what I'll see. Something is wrong with this baby. Really wrong like he might die. He can't die.

The hill is steep, the air is thick, my lungs are bursting. Past the switchback. The water tower. Gulls scatter out of my way.

"The back way! Go the back way!" someone yells.

"How do I get in?" The words come choking out of my

mouth. I hear them as if someone else has said them. I've seen Doc Ollie go into the cell house here. But how can I get in?

Somebody's there now. Up ahead. Somebody will help me. A baby can't die while I'm holding him.

"Moose!" My dad's voice, then Mr. Mattaman's. Somebody else's too. They rush toward me and sweep me through the entrance. One, two, three doors open. Stairs appear. I can't stop running, don't stop, don't let go.

There are walls made of bars. The smell of bandages. More bars.

And then I see him. The big roun gray-haired man in his clean white uniform. "Doc Ollie!" I gasp. "He's not breathing."

In the narrow hospital room, Doc takes Rocky from me. He flips him on his back on the narrow cot.

"Jimmy said he may have swallowed something. That right?" Doc Ollie asks.

"Yes."

"What was it?" I shake my head, gasping, doubled over from the pain in my side. "I dunno."

Doc Ollie props open Rocky's jaws with a bent tongue depressor.

"I didn't see," I wheeze. "I think Theresa gave him something . . . to play with."

Doc Ollie flips down the silver magnifier on his head. He looks in Rocky's throat, takes a long pair of silver forceps, and gently pulls Rocky's propped-open mouth toward him.

Ollie cocks Rocky's chin this way and that, then firmly brings the forceps down his gullet, wiggles them slightly, his eye squinting in the magnifier. "Okay, okay, don't move now, little guy, don't move. Just a little, yes!" He pulls the forceps out and Rocky begins to howl.

"Woo." Doc Ollie rocks back on his heels, lets out a huge sigh. Then he opens his hand and shows us one shiny Lincoln head penny. "Here's the culprit, right here."

9. THAT YOUR BOY, BOSS?

■ ■

Thursday, August 15, 1935

Mr. Mattaman is holding his baby son as gently as he can while Rocky howls.

"That's okay, little feller. You go ahead and give us heck." Doc Ollie smiles his big reliable smile. "It's when they don't yell you worry. Gonna have a mighty big sore throat. Don't suppose it's fun having those forceps stuck down a tiny larynx like that. Would have had the right size on hand, if I'da known you was coming."

Rocky's hollering so loud I bet they can hear him clear over on Angel Island. His little face is red as a comic book devil.

"He sure didn't like that," my dad says. "Can't say I blame him."

I'm making agreeing noises but I'm hardly listening to what he's saying, because it's suddenly occurred to me . . . I'm standing *inside* the cell house hospital!

Two long rows of cells mirror each other. Our cell has been converted to Doc Ollie's office with glass canisters filled with syringes, cotton balls, wooden sticks. Slings hang from a hook, a wheelchair with a cane seat is parked in the corner, and crutches of different sizes lean against the wall.

"Poor little guy, he's mad as a hornet. I'm gonna give him a little whiskey and milk. Let him sleep it off," Ollie says as he searches through a glass-faced cabinet.

"Thanks, Ollie." Mr. Mattaman steals a glance up from his baby son. His voice is steady, but his chin is puckered from all he's holding back.

Doc Ollie pats my shoulder with his big soft hand. "Good work there, son. Hives didn't slow you down any I'm glad to see. That salve help?"

I'm too stunned to do much else but nod, although the answer is no.

"Cam . . ." Ollie tips his head, like he's pointing with it out the door. "You reckon this boy of yours deserves a little treat?"

My dad holds the cell door open. "Ollie thinks I should give you a tour."

"A tour *of the cell house?*"

He half laughs at this. "Not the cell house, no sir. If I took you down Broadway Warden Williams would give me my walking papers."

Broadway is what they call the center row of the cell house. Even the littlest kid on Alcatraz knows this. Janet Trixle's fairy prison has a Broadway too.

"But that doesn't mean I don't have my own little surprise." My dad smiles now, clearly pleased with himself.

I follow my father down the hospital corridor with cells on one side and cells on the other. Each one is painted mint green with four cots scooted against the walls or side by side in the center. It smells vaguely of shoe polish and bleach and something acid like pee. The cells are all empty at first, then, as we walk deeper into the building, I see men sitting on beds, hanging against the bars, all of them wearing prison blue shirts, all of them watching me.

They're the ones in prison, but I'm the one being stared at like a zoo animal. I don't like this.

My father stops near the bars of a cell on the west side. Just one man in this cell, a big beefy guy with dark black hair, dark eyes, a round face, big lips, and the kind of smile that makes you like him without thinking twice about it. He's got shoe polish and a buffing rag on his bed along with a pair of shiny black guard's shoes.

The man stands up and sticks his pudgy hand through the bars. In the shadow of his left side a jagged line cuts across his face—a scar. "That your boy, boss?" he asks.

My father nods. "Moose, meet Al Capone."

I take hold Capone's hand. His handshake is firm, solid, trustworthy. I squeeze his hand with more strength than I planned. My mouth opens. "Thank you" pops out. As soon as the words hit my ears, the temperature in my face rises.

Capone smiles his broad, warm smile and chuckles deep in his throat. "He's thanking me, boss."

My father frowns. "Say hello, Moose."

"Hello," I parrot like I'm Natalie.

Capone points in the direction of Doc Ollie's office. "I heard you brought the Mattaman baby in. He doin' okay?"

"Looks that way." My father points his toothpick toward the shoes. "Who you doin' those for?"

"Officer Trixle," Capone says. "Got me a special touch. You know that."

My father snorts his disapproval.

"They like to tell people their shoes been shined up all nice by me. Looks like yours need some shining there, boss. Could do your boy's too." Capone winks at me.

"No thanks," my father answers.

Capone seems to take this in. "They gonna give me a roommate in here, boss?"

"Wouldn't know 'bout that."

"Just as soon be on my own. One or two guys don't like me too much."

"Like I said, I don't know. Depends on who's sick," my father says.

"Is that so?" Capone stares hard at my dad. "Seems to me a man's got as much power as he can wrap his mind around."

"Is that how it seems to you?"

"You bet. And I've done good for myself. I don't mind saying."

"Until now."

Capone chuckles. "Minor setback. Now your boy here . . . he don't know his own strength, but he sure can keep his head on straight when the pressure is on." He points at me with his big beefy hand. "When I get out, you look me up. I got a job waiting for you."

"He will do no such thing," my father snarls.

Al laughs a good long laugh, deep down in his belly. "Don't you worry, boss. You got yourself a good boy there. Kinda person keeps up his end of a deal." Al leans in so close the bars press against his face. "I'd be mighty proud if you were my boy," he says.

"Say goodbye, Moose," my father barks, stepping between Capone and me.

"Goodbye, Mr. Capone," I say to Al's big beaming face. I turn and follow my father down the hallway, the smell of shoe polish strong in my nose.

I'm almost out of Capone's sight when I hear it. The words drift to me in a whispery voice. "Bye, son," he says.

10. A DANGEROUS GAME

■ ■

Thursday, August 15, 1935

It isn't until I'm heading down the cell house hospital stairs into the fresh air that it really hits me. I just met Al Capone, the most powerful gangster ever to live. He called me *son*!

My skin tingles as my mind replays all of his words. *Seems to me a man's got as much power as he can wrap his mind around.* He was talking about my dad. He thought my dad had the power to make sure he didn't have a cellmate.

And that other bit about a person who keeps up his end of things? That was a message for me. He expects me to get his wife flowers. No doubt about that.

My father looks at me. "It's a shame he went bad. Could have used somebody like that on our side. Who knows, he might have been mayor, president even."

"He'da got my vote," I admit.

"I noticed that." My dad motions with his head toward the cell house. "You gotta watch the cons like him—the ones with brains. Starts innocent enough. He shines your shoes. Pretty soon, he wants a little something for his efforts. A stick of gum maybe. You gonna give it to him? Well, you owe him now. . ." He sucks his cheek in, watches a pelican fly over our heads. "Maybe you say no and he tells you, get the gum or he'll make certain the warden finds out he's been shining your shoes. So you get him his gum. Now he has two things on you. What does he do then? He ups the ante . . . that's what."

I'm shrinking. I have lost eight inches in height and begun to sweat so much my skin is slippery clear down to my shoes. My father has nailed me and he doesn't even know it.

"Moral of the story?" my father continues. "Shine your own shoes, you don't have to worry about any of that." He smiles at me.

"What about Trixle?" I ask in a wobbly voice.

My father cracks his neck. "Doesn't mean it has to happen that way. Seven Fingers gets his chocolate bars. Trixle gets his shoes shined. It's a dangerous game is all I'm saying."

"Yes, sir," I whisper.

My father's face registers concern. "Didn't mean to scare you, son. I won't let you get in trouble. Don't you worry." He pats my back reassuringly, which only makes me feel ten times worse.

I'm not the kid he can protect anymore.

"That was a good thing you did, getting Rocky up there so quick, Moose . . . you know that?"

I clear my throat, try to get ahold of myself. "Thanks," I mutter as Theresa comes tearing around the steps that lead to the front entrance of the cell house. "Moose! Mr. Flanagan! Rocky! Is Rocky okay?"

"He's okay, sweetie. Just fine," my father calls back. "Don't you worry. Your dad will be out in a few minutes."

"Are you sure?" Theresa demands, panting hard when she catches up with us.

My father pats her messy black hair. "I'm sure, little one. I saw him with my own eyes."

Theresa nods like she's taking this all in. "And my dad's coming?" Her voice gets hoarse.

"Yes," my father answers.

Theresa's little face screws up with the effort of closing her eyes so tightly. She turns on her heel and runs back down the switchback.

My father frowns as we watch her run past Piper, who is on her way up. "What was that all about?"

"I dunno," I tell him.

Piper's taking big angry steps, her hands crossed in front of her. She has a fierce expression like she's been chewing chain link.

"I think you got another problem here, Moose." My father nods toward Piper. "She's a wild one. Think I'll let you handle her on your own. Good luck with it." He winks at me and pats my arm, barely concealing his grin as he turns and heads down the hill.

"You got to go into the cell house, didn't you?" Piper asks when my father is gone.

"Sort of."

"Sort of? You either did or you didn't."

There's no way to keep this from Piper. You can't pick your teeth on this island without everyone knowing exactly what you dug out.

"C'mon, what did you see?" she demands.

I bite the inside of my cheek. "Capone," I whisper.

"No! NO! I hate you so much! It's all your fault, too, Jimmy!" Piper shouts down the switchback to Jimmy, who is heading our way.

Jimmy runs the rest of the way up to us. "What's my fault?" he asks between breaths. He leans over like he has a side ache.

"Moose met Capone." Piper glares at Jimmy. "MOOSE! He's so slow. Rocky could have died with Moose carrying him. Moose is so clumsy he could have dropped him. So why'd you let him carry your stupid brother?"

"He didn't drop him." Jimmy's voice is quiet.

"Yeah, well he could have," Piper roars.

"Yeah, well he didn't," Jimmy spits back, "and everything worked out okay."

"I'm gonna kill Theresa. *She's* the one. I can't believe you got to meet him." Piper is standing an inch away from Jimmy, blasting him down.

Jimmy does not back up. "She didn't do anything."

"Heck she didn't. She shoved me out of the way," Piper insists.

"Look, Piper . . . Rocky's fine, I didn't drop him, and they'd never have let you meet Capone anyway. In case you haven't noticed, you're a girl," I tell her as gently as I can.

"You're a kid and they let you in," Piper says.

"All I did is say hello to Al, so don't get so burned up."

"*Al*, is it? You're his *buddy* now? What did you say to him?"

I shrug. "Hello. I said hello."

Piper gets up close to me now and shouts in my face. "You met Al Capone and all you said was hello?"

"What would you have said?"

"Something a lot better than hello."

"Piper, nobody planned this, okay? It just happened. The important thing is Rocky's fine. He could have *died*," I tell her.

Piper shoves me hard. "Oh, don't be stupid. Babies don't die."

Jimmy glares at her.

"What's the matter with you? Of course they do," I tell her.

"The one chance in the whole universe to meet Capone and *you* hog it!" She shoves me again.

"Okay, okay, I'm sorry, jeez," I say, but Piper already has her back turned to me. She's stomping up the hill toward her house.

I turn to Jimmy for support, but his lips are twisted like he's trying hard to keep his feelings in. "You're *sorry*?" he asks. "You save my brother and you get to meet Capone and you're sorry?"

"I just don't want Piper mad. When she gets mad, she makes trouble. You know she does."

Jimmy snorts. "That's right. Got to keep *everybody* happy, right, Moose?"

"C'mon, Jim." I search his face trying to figure out why he's so burned up at me. "You're still sore about Scout?"

"I was never sore about Scout," Jimmy says. "He's not my friend. Why would I care what he does?"

"What do you want me to say here, Jimmy?"

"You just saved my baby brother, you don't have to say anything," he sputters, but his eyes won't engage with mine.

"Then why are you all steamed up?"

He looks up at me like he's searching for something he lost a long time ago. "The guys at my school are just like Scout. You can't play ball, you're no one," he whispers, his voice strained. "You're the only guy who likes what I like. It's kind of important, you know?"

"Okay," I tell him, "I know."

11. A ROOMFUL OF WIND-UP TOYS

· ·

Friday, August 16, 1935

The next day when I come in from the parade grounds, my mom pounces on me. "Hi, sweetheart," she says. I take a step back.

She waits for me to look inside the icebox, check the breadbox, open the cake plate, and mop up the stray crumbs.

"Last piece is yours," she offers.

I'm wolfing it down on the way to my room when she starts in. "You know I've been meaning to talk to you about something. Natalie would really appreciate a visit. She's been asking about you."

"She's coming home next month, right?"

"Look." She puts her hands up, her nostrils flare. "I know you have a lot going on, what with your baseball and your friends here on the island."

"And she doesn't have anything," I mumble.

"I didn't say that, Moose."

"You don't have to," I tell her.

My dad comes out of his room. He takes one look at us and seems to recognize trouble is brewing. "Did I miss something here?"

My mom and I look at him.

"When are you going to visit your sister?" he asks, guessing what we are discussing and automatically taking my mom's side. He pours himself a glass of lemonade. "She misses you, Moose."

"It hasn't been that long." I already feel cornered.

"No, it hasn't," my father agrees. "But we would like you to visit."

How do I tell my parents I don't like to go to Nat's schools? The teachers talk to guys my age like they're toddlers. And the kids never stop moving and swaying like a room full of wind-up toys each with its own weird rotation.

It could be me in there. Locked up that way.

I got lucky. Natalie didn't.

But it's more than that. I risked everything for the Esther P. Marinoff School. It has to be perfect. I can't stand it if it's not.

If only I could tell them what I've done for Natalie. If only they knew. Then they'd be sorry for making me feel like a heel just because I don't want to visit this one stupid time.

Since Nat's been gone, my mom goes up to the Officers' Club and plays the piano every night. She spends the time she isn't teaching playing music at the Officers' Club or cards with Mrs. Mattaman and Bea Trixle and Mrs. Caconi. My mom never even knew how to play bridge, and now she talks my father's ear off about it. And me? I come and go as I please. I never have to think about anyone but myself.

"I'll go, Mom, okay? You know I will."

"I appreciate that. Your dad and I both do. More than you know. And Natalie . . . "

"Cut it out, Mom," I say more firmly than I planned. "I said I'd go, okay?"

"Okay," she whispers. "Okay."

12. THE IRISH WAY

■ ■

Saturday, August, 17, 1935

I stay in my room for the rest of that day and all of the next, reading *The Definitive History of Baseball*. There's nothing like *The Definitive History of Baseball* to make you feel better when the clock is ticking and only in a matter of hours you'll be hunted down by a guy with a shotgun in his violin case, because you can't figure out how to get yellow roses to Big Al's wife. And if that's not bad enough, your best friend on Alcatraz and your best baseball-playing friend on Alcatraz and the girl you're sweet on are all mad at you for reasons that make no sense at all. Plus you just got more hives on your leg, and the itching is driving you buggy and you just may scratch the skin off your leg so you'll be skinless sometime soon.

I guess when you're dead it doesn't matter if you have skin or not.

This does not make me feel better.

I'm in the middle of reading how the shoes of a pitcher named Joe were rubbing his blisters, so he played in his socks and after that they called him Shoeless Joe Jackson, when I hear a knock on our front door.

"Moose, mind if I come in?" Mrs. Mattaman calls out.

"Come on in, Mrs. Mattaman," I answer. This is the first

good news I've had in two days. Mrs. Mattaman never visits without baked goods in her hand.

She sets a whole plate of cannolis on my bookshelf and smiles, clearly pleased at my reaction. "We're awful grateful, Mr. Mattaman and me," she says, sitting on my bed, which squeaks like a rusty bike.

"I feel like a big fool here, Moose, after all you've done . . . but I've come to ask for something else." Her hair is neater and her face is more mature than Theresa's, but her eyes are just as lively—*full of the dickens*, my mother would say.

Mrs. Mattaman balls up a corner of her apron. "Jimmy knows he should have watched Rocky more closely. But he's not going to go making himself sick over it. But my little girl, she takes everything hard. I know she'd never have hurt that baby. I know it was an accident. But Theresa—" Mrs. Mattaman sighs. "She can't forgive herself for giving that penny to Rocky. She's in bed now. Been there for two straight days. Won't come out for love nor money.

"Everybody makes mistakes. You try and learn from them is all, get a little more information in your noggin." She taps her brain. "So you know better the next time."

"You want me to tell Theresa that?"

"My Theresa thinks the world of you, Moose. Course you Irish have a way about you. Don't think I haven't noticed." She wags her finger at me. "But if Theresa thought you needed her really badly for something—"

"Oh . . . like what?"

She throws her hands in the air. "Whatever it is you kids are always so busy doing. Come talk to her, will you?" she asks, sucking her lips inside her mouth like Theresa does.

I follow Mrs. Mattaman to her apartment. On the way, I see Jimmy down at the dock, tracking our progress. When he sees that I see him, his head ducks down as if he wasn't watching. Here I am, stepping on his toes again. But what am I supposed to do? This was Mrs. Mattaman's idea, not mine.

Why is it people always ask me to do these things anyway?

Theresa is completely under the white nubby bedcover. Not even a toe is sticking out—it's just one big Theresa-size lump planted in the middle of her bed.

"Hey Theresa . . . c'mon, stick your head out, I gotta talk to you," I say.

"Theresa isn't here," she whispers.

"Well, hmmm," I say, "this is definitely Theresa's room. I wonder where Theresa went?"

The lump is silent.

Out in the living room, Mrs. Mattaman switches the station on the radio. It makes a patchwork of high-pitched squeaks until she settles on Jack Benny.

I try again. "Look, I heard Annie wants to put together some more gangster cards. She really needs your help. Nobody knows how many bullet holes to put in Bonnie and Clyde except you."

Still nothing. Not even a change in the wrinkle pattern over her little self.

I look around her room. What am I going to do here? If Mrs. Mattaman can't figure this out, then how am I supposed to?

Where is Theresa's strange stuff on Alcatraz book? I wonder. Maybe there's something in that. Once she was sure Baby Face Nelson was hiding in the canteen pickle barrel. Another time she thought she'd found Al Capone's pinky ring, but it was a clasp that fell off of Bea Trixle's purse.

On her bedside table is a pad of paper. Maybe I'll write her a note and send it under the covers. I flip through looking for a blank sheet. "Dear Theresa," I begin on a page with a faint impression of a checkerboard. I know what this was from. Theresa drew a checkerboard so that she could play button checkers with Natalie.

Theresa understands Natalie better than any other little kid ever has. She's able to figure out how to play with her too.

"I'm going to visit Natalie tomorrow," I blurt out.

Just as my lips form these words, a plan begins to take shape in my mind. I could go to San Francisco to visit Natalie and then make certain I got on the 2:00 boat, the ferry Mae will be taking. Theresa could come with me. Seven-year-old little girls can get away with things that almost-thirteen-year-old boys cannot. Theresa could just hand Mae the roses . . . couldn't she?

"I need help." My voice comes out in an urgent rush. "Will you come?"

The Theresa lump moves a smidgen. The covers rearrange around her middle.

"I have to talk to Mr. Purdy, the headmaster. You could play button checkers with Natalie. That way you can keep her busy while I talk."

"Bring a magazine," Theresa whispers.

"Sure, but once she presses her face on each page, she's done with the magazine. My talk with Mr. Purdy's gonna run much longer than that."

"Bring an index. You don't need me."

"I can't read to her and talk to Mr. Purdy at the same time."

"She's there without me all the time," Theresa growls.

"Yeah, but not when I'm there. If I spend my time talking to Purdy, she's not gonna like that."

Silence again, but there's a different feel to this silence, like maybe Theresa is thinking about this.

I tap the flat part of the bedspread near what I think is Theresa's leg. "Natalie is going to expect you to be there. What am I going to tell her?"

This elicits a big complicated sigh from the white bedcover. "Tell her I'm stupid. Tell her I'm the stupidest person in the whole world and she's lucky I'm not there."

"Theresa, you're not stupid. You made a mistake. I make mistakes all the time. I made at least 150 mistakes in the last hour. Wait no, 151."

Theresa's voice is so quiet I almost don't hear it. "He almost died."

"Yeah and you did the right thing. You let Jimmy and me know he was in trouble and we got him to Doc Ollie and Doc Ollie got the penny out. And now he's fine."

More silence.

"I wished Rocky would go away." She can hardly get these words out.

"Yeah, okay," I whisper back. "But that doesn't mean you don't love him. Do you know how many times I've wished Natalie would go away?" As soon as I say this my armpits begin to sweat and my hives burn. I don't mean this. I don't.

"Really?" Theresa whispers, her voice yearning.

My hand steadies myself on the bed. I can't lie to Theresa,

but I sure as heck don't want to talk about this. "Sometimes I feel that way," I admit.

The covers are moving, like she is nodding.

"But Natalie's not going to understand any of this. All she'll know is you aren't there."

"I'm a jinx," Theresa says.

"No, you're not."

"Am so. That's what Piper said."

"Since when do you listen to her?"

"Since never," she concedes.

"Exactly. Piper is full of crap. You of all people know that."

The covers move again in a nodding motion. "Why do you like her then?" Theresa whispers.

"I never said I did."

"You do, though."

"It's a small island. We all have to get along."

"You *like* her!" Theresa's voice is strong now.

"Right now I don't."

This gets her. She sits up straight in bed and takes her covers off. "Why? What did she do?"

"She . . ." I stare into Theresa's disheveled face. "Look, I'll be there tomorrow on the ten a.m. I need you to come, okay? I really do."

Theresa doesn't answer, but I can tell by the way her eyes are looking straight up, as if to see what's in her own head, that's she's thinking about this.

Boy, do I hope she decides to come.

13. EVERYBODY LIKES MOOSE

....

Sunday, August 18, 1935

The next morning I head straight for the dock, the *Definitive History of Baseball* under my arm and all the money my grandma ever sent me for my birthday in my pocket. I think about stopping by the Mattamans' on the way down, but I decide against it. My dad says when it comes to girls the fastest route from A to B is hardly ever the best one.

Once I'm down at the dock, I begin to stew. What if Theresa doesn't come? Luckily, it isn't long before I see her dark uncombed head poke out of her front door, her church coat and hat in her hand. She's got to be coming with me.

But wait. What's she doing now? She's going upstairs, not down. Uh-oh. She's not headed for Annie's house . . . is she?

She is.

Theresa's decided not to come? But then why is she wearing her good clothes? Okay, she's back outside now, tugging on Annie's arm. Annie has her church clothes on too.

Annie's coming? Uh-oh. And what's Annie have with her? A bag with her baseball bat sticking out of it. She's wearing her church clothes and she has her baseball gear?

By the time they get down to the dock, Jimmy appears. He must have been watching from the canteen. "Where are you going?" Jimmy asks Annie and Theresa.

"Gonna visit Natalie," I tell him.

"Me too, and Annie's coming, aren't you, Annie?" Theresa smiles up at her.

"I thought you were never leaving your room," Jimmy mutters.

"I had to," Theresa explains. "Moose needs my help, don't you, Moose?"

"And you?" Jimmy's eyes dart to Annie. His tongue pokes his cheek out of shape. "You got your baseball gear?"

"Don't look at me," I say. " I have no idea why she's bringing her baseball gear." "Like I believe that," Jimmy says.

"I don't," I insist, watching a gull land with a live crab in its mouth. The bird sets the crab down gently, then snaps a leg off and swallows it.

"I thought I'd just see, you know, if he was at the field," Annie explains.

"*He,* meaning Scout?" Jimmy asks.

"Scout's not going to be there," I tell Annie.

"How do you know?" Annie asks.

"I just do," I explain, watching the gull snap another leg off the still-moving crab.

Annie grinds her teeth. Her lids lower on her pop-out eyes. "You just don't want me to play with him."

"I don't want you to pull a stunt like you did the last time, if that's what you mean."

She shrugs, her eyes focused on her trousers, which I see she is wearing under her dress. "I can't stop you from playing in the city."

"You can't stop me? What's that supposed to mean?" I ask.

Annie shrugs. "It was for your own good what I did. But maybe I know more now."

"What are you talking about?" Theresa demands.

Annie looks over the top of Theresa's head. "I'm just looking out for you."

"Sure doesn't feel that way," I say as the gull swallows the crab's legless body whole. Is this what Capone's hit men are going to do to me?

The boarding whistle blows.

"Look, go get your gear. Hurry or we'll miss the boat!" Annie puts on her bossy voice.

"Yeah, Moose, hurry," Jimmy echoes dryly.

No way I'll be playing ball today. I'm just hoping I don't end up like that poor crab, eaten alive one leg at a time. Still, I go get my gear. I never say no to baseball. On the way up to my apartment, I try to sort out this mess. How am I going to get roses for Mae if Annie's with me? How am I going to get back on the 2:00 boat with Theresa and the flowers if we go to visit Natalie and then go to the Marina to play with Scout?

I should have told Annie she couldn't come with us because Natalie isn't allowed that many visitors. Is it too late for this? I could say I forgot this rule. People forget . . . don't they? Then maybe Jim won't be so mad because he won't feel so left out.

This is a good plan I decide. But when I get back to the boat, Jimmy is gone and my father, in his officer's uniform, and Mrs. Mattaman, in her apron, are both standing with Theresa and Annie.

My dad pats my back. "What a good idea, Moose. Natalie will love having a whole Alcatraz contingent come visit her."

What am I going to do now? I could say my hives are

bothering me and I can't go. But then how will I get on the boat an hour later? I could send Theresa and Annie off to find Scout, while I get the roses. Or maybe I could . . . I could . . .

"Natalie's going to be pleased as punch to see you three," Mrs. Mattaman says as the key sails down the guard tower guy wire. She hands me a package all tied up with string. "You eat the others already, Moose?"

"Might have."

My father laughs.

Mrs. Mattaman's eyes glow with this information. "Glad you're not my son. Between you and Jimmy, you'd eat me out of house and home," she coos.

"You girls keep a close eye on him, okay? Make sure he saves some for Natalie." My father winks.

"Probably should have baked a lemon cake." Mrs. Mattaman winds her finger around her apron string. "You tell her I will soon as she gets home. You betcha."

"Last call ten a.m.," Trixle bellows, his bullhorn directed at us.

"You heard the man. On the double, you three." Mrs. Mattaman shoos us down the gangplank. She stands on the dock watching us as we push off. The boat rail gently moves up and down. The motor rumbles under my feet.

"My mom sure likes Moose," Theresa tells Annie.

"Everybody likes Moose," Annie says. "That's the trouble."

"Why is that the trouble?" I ask.

Annie shakes her head. "It just is."

14. DEAD TWELVE-YEAR-OLDS

▪ ▪

Same day—Sunday, August 18, 1935

The whole way to the Esther P. Marinoff School I try to plan everything out. I'm going to take Annie to the wrong field, so we don't run into Scout. I hate the idea of missing out on a pickup game, but this is my life we're talking about. I'm not sure what kind of pickup games they have in heaven. I don't think there are that many dead baseball-playing twelve-year-olds up there.

The more I think about this, the harder I work to wiggle the string off the cannoli box and worm my big hand inside. I've just managed to eat two when Annie rips the box out of my hands. "What's the matter with you, Moose?" she asks as we walk up the steep San Francisco street with the cables rumbling underground and the cable car bell clanking in the distance.

We're almost to the Esther P. Marinoff now, which is good because my legs feel wobbly, like I just climbed up twenty flights of stairs. We didn't have hills like this in Santa Monica. We didn't have mansions like this either.

On one side of the enormous white house is a large, well-cared-for garden full of flowers. Orange flowers drape from a trellis and tiny pink and purple flowers the size of a lady's thumbnail spill over the side of a planter. It smells sweet like honeysuckle. A metal placard reads in elaborate cursive *The Esther P. Marinoff School*.

I look around for roses. Just my luck, there are none.

"Es-thur. Pee. Mary-noff. Lookee, you guys! This is it!" Theresa runs around behind me and gives me a shove, head-butting me up the stairs to the massive front door. Annie laughs as I ring the doorbell and Theresa pounds on the solid oak door.

It takes a while, but eventually the big door is opened by a small woman with hair the color of tarnished nickels and a velvet dress thick as movie curtains. Her eyes are a clear gold, the color of beer.

"We're here to visit Natalie Flanagan," I tell her.

"And you are?"

"Moose, I mean Matthew Flanagan, her brother, and Theresa Mattaman and Annie Bomini, her friends."

"Ahhh, the Alcatraz kids!" The woman smiles, takes my hand in her tiny one, and pumps my arm. "I'm Sadie," she says.

Though she must be my grandma's age, there's something about her that seems young, like the graying hair and wrinkled skin are a costume change and not the real person at all. We follow her inside.

"I've heard a lot about you kids. Natalie talks about you all the—"

"Yes, ma'am." I cut her off before I can stop myself. I don't want to hear about Nat missing me while I've been home with my mom and my dad all to myself.

Sadie blinks like she has dust in her eyes. "Well then, you must be anxious to see Natalie. You wait right here. I'll bring her up."

Annie's watchful blue eyes take everything in. The room reminds me of Sadie herself: full of once-elegant things that are well worn. Chairs with old-fashioned carved legs and threadbare seats. Brocade curtains, faded smooth in spots. But nothing about this place seems like gangsters, and Sadie sure doesn't look like the kind of woman who would mix it up with mobsters. How did Al Capone do it? How did he get Natalie into this school?

Theresa bounces on the lumpy seat of her straight-back chair. She jumps up when she hears the sound of Natalie approaching, dragging one foot along the carpet. Step, drag. Step, drag.

"She's here!" Theresa cries, clapping her hands together.

When Nat appears she's wearing the yellow dress my mom and the convicts made for her, but the belt is gone and there are two extra buttons sewn to the front.

For a second Nat's clear green eyes flash past me, then flip down to the carpet again.

"Sun get up okay today, Natalie?" Nat mutters.

Sadie's thick velvet dress sweeps past us. "Natalie. Look at the person with whom you're speaking. And speak in proper pronouns, please."

I don't like Sadie's tone. What gives her the right to talk to Natalie this way? "Natalie loves the sunrise. She gets up for it every morning," I explain. "When I get up, I always ask her if the sun got up okay."

"She loves the sunrise and the garden too, but she can speak more directly," Sadie informs me, her eyes trained on Nat.

"Three and oh. No hits, no runs. A fly ball. Ten base hits.

A runner on third," Natalie mumbles, digging her chest with her chin.

Sadie cups her hand under Natalie's chin to prevent the digging. "No baseball talk," she says.

"What's the matter with baseball talk?" I ask.

"She's just repeating random phrases. We're working on the art of conversation," Sadie explains. "Say what you mean. I am . . ." Sadie prompts Natalie.

Natalie tries to dig at her chest again, but Sadie's hand won't let her chin dip down. Nat looks quickly and fleetingly across the tops of our heads. "Moose, Theresa, Annie hello, hello, hello," Nat mutters.

"Hi, Natalie," we all say.

"You have new buttons." Theresa points to the two extra mismatched buttons sewn to Natalie's dress.

Natalie runs her hands over the new buttons, carefully, lovingly, tracing the outline of each one. "Good day new button," she whispers.

"Who are you addressing, Natalie?" Sadie barks. "When I have . . ."

Nat doesn't respond.

Sadie motions for us to be silent. We wait a painfully long time and then suddenly Nat offers: "When I have a Sadie nice day, I get a new button."

"Good, Natalie!" Sadie's voice is buoyant.

Nat rubs her hand over one of her sewn-on buttons.

"Maybe you'll get more buttons," Annie offers. "When you come home next weekend, maybe you'll have more."

"More buttons, more," Natalie repeats. "I am—"

"I am what?" Sadie pounces on this beginning. Her face is

up close to Nat's.

But Natalie lets it drop. Whatever she is right now, she isn't going to say.

"What we're working on here, Moose," Sadie explains, "is keeping her engaged and a part of the conversation. We can't let her float off into her own world."

"She doesn't float off in her own world *with me*," Theresa says proudly.

Sadie smiles. "You're the neighbor girl, right?"

Theresa beams. "Do you want to play button checkers?" she asks Natalie, laying out her hand-drawn checkerboard.

Natalie touches each button as Theresa sets it out. When she finishes, she starts again, following the exact same pattern of touching as before. When she's done, she nods, almost to herself, and she and Theresa play.

After Natalie has won two games—even with our coaching, Theresa is no match for her—she begins twisting the buttons on her dress one way, then the other.

"I am—I am—" Nat's voice is stiff with unnatural pauses. She drags her toe against the carpet and against the carpet again. Her eyes move back and forth in her head like she's trying to make the room spin away.

Sadie looks up from her paperwork. "I am what?" she asks.

"I am . . . Natalie angry," Nat says in the same mechanical way.

"She says she's angry," Theresa explains.

"I am angry," Sadie corrects.

"I am angry," Natalie repeats.

"Yes, you surely are," Sadie says, her eyes keen and clear on Natalie. "Who are you angry with?"

Natalie's head goes down again. She pinches the skin of her arm. "Angry at Mommy. Angry at Moose," she spits.

"Me? What did I do?" I ask.

Nat doesn't answer.

"You made her say that," I tell Sadie before I can stop myself.

"I did nothing of the kind," Sadie replies.

"Moose," Annie warns in a low voice.

"Why is she angry?" I ask.

"You just left her in this place," Annie murmurs.

"Yeah, but it's for her own good," I shoot back defensively.

"Doesn't mean she won't be angry," Annie explains.

"Okay, okay," I say. "But I don't think she's really mad *at me*."

"I sure would be mad at you if you sent me away." Theresa makes puppy dog eyes.

"You don't understand," I insist.

"We ask an awful lot of our students here, Moose." Sadie neatens her stack of paperwork. "When you've spent your whole life one way, it isn't easy to change. We are proud of how well Natalie is doing with us. She's made a remarkable start."

"Yeah," Annie whispers, "she has."

"She's trying. I hope you see that. Part of what we're striving for here is to give Natalie a way to control herself. Because once those blades inside her get to spinning, it's just too hard for her to stop herself."

"Why is she mad at *me* though?" I demand. "Natalie never gets mad at me. Natalie, you never get mad at me," I tell her.

"Natalie never gets mad at me," Natalie echoes.

"Use your words, Natalie. *Your* words, not someone else's. I

. . . I . . ." Sadie opens her mouth and enunciates in a way that makes me want to slap her face.

"Moose . . ." Nat dips her chin down before Sadie can stop her. "Moose, I missed Moose," she says in a voice so low I almost don't hear it.

15. MAE CAPONE IS A LOOKER

■■■■■■■■■■■■■■■■■■■■■■■■■■■■■■■■■■■■

Same day—Sunday, August 18, 1935

We're almost to the field where Scout plays. Actually, we're almost to the field where Scout doesn't play. My plan is to see that Scout isn't there, get some roses, and somehow manage to convince Theresa to give them to Mae without Annie knowing. I try to focus on this and not on Natalie. But Nat's words have crawled inside my head: *Moose, I missed Moose.*

What was so disturbing about seeing her today was I suddenly realized how hard she was trying. I thought she didn't try. But it's much more upsetting to realize she actually does try. She tries very hard for what seems like such a small result.

I force myself to stop thinking about this. Right now I've got to figure out how to keep Al Capone from hunting me down. I can't allow myself to think about anything else.

I'm just turning my plan around in my head when two girls in white gloves and hats start waving wildly to Annie.

"Dolores! Peggy!" Annie hurries to catch up with them. The girls' heads cluster together like three birds with one cracker. They peek up at me and duck down again for more whispering.

"Is it? Is it him?" I hear one ask.

Annie blushes all the way down to the roots of her yellow-moon-colored hair.

I look around to see who they're talking about. Theresa skips over to the girls to find out what's going on.

Annie's still-pink face appears. "Moose. These are my friends Dolores"—she points to the one with buckteeth—"and Peggy." She nods to the short girl.

I raise my hand in a wooden wave and drop it again.

Dolores and Peggy smile at Annie like they're all in on a secret.

"We better get going," I tell Annie.

"Yes, you better," Peggy says. "Have fun, Annie," she giggles.

"Yeah, Annie," Dolores, the one with the buckteeth, chimes in.

Now wouldn't it be nice if Annie decided to go off with them. I can't imagine how I'll get Theresa to help me with Annie around.

No such luck. Annie stays.

How am I going to do this? I could leave the roses for Mae in the visitors' section of the boat, but with Mae Capone on board, won't there be extra officers on the *Coxe*? There always are on visitors' day, and I'll bet there will be twice as many when the visitor is Scarface's wife. Trixle will be there for certain. He'd never miss this. I can just imagine what would happen if he found the roses.

Theresa skips ahead. I walk with Annie.

"Where do you guys play exactly?" Annie asks, looking down the long expanse of grass at the Marina Green.

"On a back street a few minutes from here," I tell her.

"You know, Moose, I've been thinking . . . are you sure Al

Capone got her in that school? It doesn't look like a gangland operation to me," Annie says.

"Which would look how?" I ask, stepping off the curb to avoid the man selling apples. This is what men do when they can't get work. If I got caught, would this happen to my father?

"More silk and whiskey. Glamorous stuff . . . you know. No way Capone had anything to do with that place."

"Maybe not. I don't know if I like the place, anyway. I don't like it when they put words in her mouth," I confess.

"You just didn't like what Natalie had to say. The place is good for her, Moose. Trust me," Annie says.

Trust her, *right*. Everybody thinks they know what's best for Natalie: religion, leafy green vegetables, stricter discipline, ice compresses, voodoo. I've heard it all. But wait a minute, if Annie thinks the Esther P. Marinoff School is the right place for Natalie, maybe she'll have changed her mind about telling.

"So you don't want to wreck it for Natalie?" My voice squeaks hopefully.

"It was a mistake is all. That's what I think," Annie declares. "I heard my dad talking to my Uncle Tony when we drove down to San Mateo yesterday. I was in the rumble seat. They thought I was asleep. My dad said he played chess with Buddy Boy when Buddy was in the hospital. Buddy's a great chess player and so is my dad."

Guards aren't supposed to play chess with inmates. That I know for sure.

"They had to be quiet, so they passed notes to let each other know stuff. *Done. Your turn.* Doesn't that sound like the kind of notes you pass in a game? They must have gotten in your laundry by mistake."

"Maybe," I reply, scratching a hive on my elbow. I would have totally believed it was possible if I hadn't received the note about Mae and the roses. There's no way *that* was about a chess game, but I'm not about to tell Annie this. "Who won?" I ask.

"Buddy." Annie's eyes are hopeful. "I think it was all an accident," she confides.

I look up from where I've been clawing my elbow. "So you'll play baseball with me on Alcatraz?" I ask.

Annie squints at me. "You haven't gotten any other notes, have you?"

I can't lie about this. Not to Annie. I look down the quiet backstreet. A ragman calls in the distance. A milkman knocks on a door. A cluster of girls plays jacks on the street. "This is where we play," I announce.

"*Here?*" Annie is incredulous.

"I told you he wouldn't be here today," I say, hoping Annie won't notice I didn't answer her question about the notes.

Theresa bounces back to us. "If he's not here, we should go find him. Can we, Moose? Can we?"

"There's no time," I tell Theresa. "I gotta get back. I promised my mom. And I have to buy flowers."

Theresa's mouth pulls to one side. "But we woulda had time to play though. That would have taken time," she reasons.

"Yeah, but Scout lives pretty far from here. We don't have time to go get him and then play." I'm pleased with how this comes out. It sounds like I know what I'm talking about.

"You're going to buy flowers? For Piper?" Annie asks.

I'd planned to say my mom, but suddenly Piper sounds like a better idea, mostly because I have never in my life bought my mom flowers. Not that I'd buy them for Piper, but it does seem more likely.

This lying business is a lot more complicated than it looks.

"Yeah," I say.

"Ohhhhh!" Theresa's eyes seek Annie's.

"It's a good idea," Annie tells me. "She's mad at you, you know. Maybe flowers will help."

"Tell me about it," I say.

"Don't worry. She's mad at the world right now. My mom says it's because she's been the apple in her dad's eye and now all he ever talks about is how much he wants a son. Piper won't do well as second fiddle." The corners of Annie's mouth sneak up a little.

"So where are we getting the flowers?" Theresa wants to know.

"Let's walk down Union. Probably a flower stand there."

We walk about six blocks and don't find anything. So Annie goes into a butcher shop and asks. The butcher directs us to a small stand, no bigger than an outhouse. They have roses: red, yellow, and pink. My gut pinches when I see how expensive they are. How can something you can just pick cost so much? I don't have enough for a dozen, but I can buy a half dozen. Will that be enough?

"What color?" Annie asks.

"Yellow," I tell the man behind the counter.

"I'd go with red. Yellow is friendship. Red is, *you know* . . ." Annie moves her almost-white eyebrows up and down.

"That's why I want yellow," I insist.

Carefully I take my bat, ball, and glove out of the bag and set the yellow roses inside. I don't want Darby Trixle or any of the other officers to see I'm carrying them. I wonder if Annie will comment about this, but she doesn't say a word.

The closer we get to the water, the worse my hives itch. Even Annie notices. "What are you scratching so much for? You allergic to flowers?" Annie asks.

"Hey look." Theresa points to the dock at Fort Mason where we catch the boat back to Alcatraz. Maybe fifty or a hundred people are milling around like ants in a sugar bowl. A man standing on a barrel waves his arms and calls out. "Mae Capone, the wife of public enemy number one. She's right here, folks. Don't miss this. Gonna visit her hubby on the Rock. She's quite the beauty too. C'mon, folks, Mae Capone right here."

Theresa grabs my arm. "Did you hear that? Mae Capone! C'mon!"

But I'm not thinking about Mae. I'm thinking about Al. The man is stark raving mad. How am I supposed to give his wife flowers with all these people around? The place is swarming with reporters. They'd probably snap my picture as I give them to her. Then I'll be in the morning papers. That's just what I need. The warden would fire my father in a heartbeat t.

I can't get Theresa to hand Mae the roses either. If her picture gets in the paper, she'll get in trouble, same as I would. Didn't Scarface know Mae would be mobbed like this?

A reporter in a gray suit leans toward us. He hands out business cards like he's dealing from a deck. "You kids live on Alcatraz? What's the word on Capone? We heard he's got his own furniture up there, Oriental rugs and the whole nine yards."

"Capone gonna bust right outta there. You heard it from me," the man on the barrel shouts.

A man with a puffy nose waves his big hand in my face. "You live on the Rock?" He shoves a slip of paper at me as a guy stinking of cigarettes hurries past.

"A hot tip's worth cash money to me." A guy with hairy wrists folds my hand around his card.

"We can't, sir. The warden won't let us talk to reporters—" Annie tells him as the crowd presses in.

"She's coming!" Theresa shouts. My pulse is growing louder like my own heart is getting closer to me.

A man scrambles over the back of another. A large woman picks a reporter up and moves him out of her way. A guy with a hat two sizes too small is shooting photos in a mad rush. Another man in a dark suit elbows in front of me.

"This is crazy. Let's get on the boat." Annie pulls Theresa and me past the buck sergeant, who checks us off on his clipboard. We scoot up the ramp and out of the fray. Back onto the boat, settling against the railing, we see the tops of everyone's heads as they rush Mae Capone.

Mae hides behind her mink wrap, and her leather gloves cover what little of her face isn't buried in mink. A hat with a brown veil sits smartly on her short platinum blond movie star hair. I can't hardly see her, but one thing is clear.

Mae Capone is a looker.

Shee's making her way up the gangplank, but it's slow going.

"How's he doin'? His life in danger? What can you tell us, Mrs. Capone?"

And then from the back of the crowd Warden Williams appears, flanked by three Angel Island army officers.

Oh great, this is just who I need . . . . the warden!

"Gentlemen! Gentlemen! Give the lady some room, please," the warden's booming voice barks. The people nearest the warden seem to sense the power shift and they take a reluctant step back.

What am I supposed to do now, give Mae roses in front of the warden? It kind of explains why Piper isn't here though. She must have known he'd be on the boat.

"They like the big guy on Alcatraz? They treating him right?" One man in the back keeps at it.

Another officer positions his barrel chest between Mae and the reporters. A skeleton-thin man throws a fistful of cards her way. "Floyd's the name, at the *Examiner*. I'll make it worth your while."

But the warden is on him now. He picks up the cards and hands them back. "These won't be necessary, Mr. Floyd," he says.

The warden and the officers have the crowd in hand now. A path clears for Mae Capone and she heads up the gangplank straight for us. Her cheeks are flushed. Her lips are like bright boysenberries. Her perfume smells of lilacs and talcum powder mixed with the dead fish at the dock. She's so close I could reach out and touch her soft brown leather glove.

I glance down at the warden still on the dock. His back is to us as he confers with one of the Angel Island officers. Mae's mink brushes past my arm. "Excuse me," Mae says.

My mouth drops open. All I can think about is giving her the roses, but I can't do that here. Not with the warden right there. What am I, nuts? Theresa jabs her elbow in my side. "Me. Oh . . . How do you do, Mrs. Capone," I stutter.

And then suddenly it occurs to me. If I give roses to every

woman on the boat, I won't get in trouble.

I grab a rose and hand it to Mae as she sweeps past. "Here. And here." I give another to Annie and one to Theresa.

Mae smiles at me, a beautiful smile. "Why, thank you . . . Moose, isn't it?" she says, and then she's gone, yellow rose in hand. flanked by the officers and Darby Trixle.

Theresa's eyes are big as Bundt cakes. "Why'd you do that?" she asks.

But I ignore Theresa as I hurry over to Doc Ollie's sister, who looks exactly like him. She even wears the high-heeled equivalent of his sturdy shoes. I give her a rose and one to Mrs. Caconi and one to Bea Trixle.

"Why, Moose!" Bea Trixle's face glows all the way down to the mouse brown roots of her Hollywood blond hair. "Isn't that the sweetest thing! What a nice young man you are! Darby! Oh, Darby!" Bea waves her husband down. "See what that nice Flanagan boy gave me." She jiggles the rose in his face.

Darby sucks on his bottom lip.

"A rose. Long-stemmed too," Bea tells Darby. "You know my birthday is coming up."

"Yes, honey bunch." Trixle glares at me. "I know."

"They couldn't be that expensive if a twelve-year-old boy got one," Bea tells him as the warden appears, walking across the deck in his deliberate manner, the boat gently swaying. He surveys the scene.

"Where did the roses come from?" the warden asks Trixle.

Trixle waggles his head in my direction. "Flanagan boy, sir."

The warden looks at me so hard it feels like he can see through my skull. "What's this business about, Matthew?" he asks, using my real name which always means trouble.

My knees are quaking under me. "Nothing, sir," I tell him, trying to force my voice through my tight throat.

"Nothing, is it?" The warden raises his eyebrows. "Quite the ladies' man, aren't you?"

"No, sir," I mutter.

"That's not what my Piper says. I have my eye on you, Flanagan." The warden shakes his head. "Got my fingers crossed the next one is a boy so I won't have to worry about the likes of Moose Flanagan," he tells Trixle.

"Ain't nothing like a boy, sir," Trixle agrees. "Me and the missus got our hopes on one too."

"For twenty years been hankering for a son." The warden smiles, his chest full, his blue eyes bright with possibility. Then he seems to realize I am still here.

"Go on, get out of here, Mr. Flanagan," the Warden tells me, and I begin to walk away but then I hear Trixle.

"It ain't Moose I worry about. It's his sister."

"She's not even on the island now, right?" the warden asks.

"Yeah, but she's comin' back, ain't that right, Moose?" Trixle raises his voice so I can hear. He clearly knows I'm listening to this.

I turn around. "Yes, sir, but we keep a close eye on her. She's never been in any trouble, sir," I tell him.

Trixle snorts. "She's a loose cannon. It's a cryin' shame' it is. Lettin' normal kids mix it up with buggy ones," Darby tells the warden. "Don't know what some people is thinking."

"Natalie's not buggy, she just thinks a different way." The words shoot out of me before I can stop them. I know my dad would not like me talking to the warden and Trixle like this.

"Is that so?" Trixle asks.

"Yes, sir." I nod to the warden. "It is."

When I get back to Annie and Theresa they're staring at me, their eyes squinting, their mouths half open. They have clearly been discussing me in my absence.

"We can't take these," Annie says, the wind whipping her hair, the rose held tightly against her chest.

"They're for Piper," Theresa scolds, leaning close so I can hear her over the wind and the rumbling motor.

"Course you can. I always meant to give them to you. I just wanted to surprise you," I tell them.

"Surprise us?" Annie cocks her head.

Theresa squints at me. She clearly doesn't believe this.

"No, really," I say, steadying myself on the boat railing.

Annie looks at the rose, holds it delicately with her hand. A smile forms on her big square lips as she smells it. "Are you sure?" she asks without looking at me.

"Sure I'm sure," I say.

"But what about Piper?" Theresa insists.

"I don't want to give Piper flowers."

Annie watches me from behind the rose. "That's not what you said," she says.

"Like I said, I wanted to surprise you."

Annie's pale cheeks are flushed. She lets her finger bump on the smooth part of the stem. She holds it safe from the wind.

"But, Moose." Theresa jabs her elbow in my side. "Mae said your name."

"She couldn't have," I tell them.

"She did though. I heard it with my own ears." Theresa

touches one of her ears as if to prove her point.

"I don't know, Theresa," I murmur with one eye on Annie. I can't tell if Annie's listening or not.

"You don't know?" Theresa's eyes are white all around. "I have to put it in my book, Moose. This is a very strange occurrence," she informs me.

I wish she wouldn't. But then most of what she writes is made up anyway. No one will think it's actually true.

In the visitors' section I see Mae Capone holding her yellow rose across her lap. Doc Ollie's old sister with her practical shoes has placed the rose behind her ear, like she's become a flamenco dancer. And there's Bea Trixle talking to Mrs. Caconi, holding the rose as if it is made of glass.

It's amazing the power of a few stupid flowers. Simply amazing.

16. PINEAPPLE UPSIDE-DOWN CAKE

. . . .

Same day— Sunday, August 18, 1935

Why, thank you Moose. The lilting sound of Mae's voice is spinning around like a gramophone inside my head. And now Darby Trixle is heading back to us. Won't he ever leave me alone?

"What you kids doin' on this run anyway?" Darby asks.

"We went to visit my sister," I tell him.

Trixle's chiseled face sets. His eyes narrow. "That it, is it? Wasn't nothin' to do with Mae Capone bein' here? The warden thinks this ain't no coincidence."

My forehead begins to sweat when I hear this. Big beads drip down.

"We didn't know she was going to be here, sir," Annie offers.

"We just we got lucky," Theresa adds.

Darby glares at her. Theresa shrinks behind Annie.

"And what about you, Mr. Ladies' Man?" He squints at me, catching himself as the boat dips in the wake of another ferry. "Just went to visit your sister, did you?"

"Yes, sir," I say.

Tsk, tsk, Darby clucks. "How's she doin' at that place?"

"Fine, sir."

"She comin' back?"

"She'll be back in two weeks."

His mouth sours up. "Ain't permanent, then, this place she's at? The one that's for *different* kids."

"It's a school, sir."

"Is that what they call it nowadays . . ." He makes a juicy noise with his spit and looks over at Theresa's rose. "And them flowers the missus is all worked up about? How much they put you back, son?"

I shrug. Best not to say anything. He's just looking for trouble, and I don't want to give it to him.

"Bet it was a lotta dough. And you just giving them away free like that? How you get that money?"

"My grandma sent it to me."

"Your grandma sent it to you and you bought my missus flowers with it, did you?"

"Not exactly . . . I bought them for Annie and Theresa and I had a few left over."

"So my missus didn't rate. She was leftovers?" He snorts.

"Well, no, I mean, um."

"Darby! Darby!" Bea is doing her best to run across the rocking boat in her high-heeled shoes while holding her scarf around her head. She shakes her finger at Darby. "Don't you be getting after that nice young man. I won't have it. Just because you aren't kind and thoughtful the way he is."

Darby's face gets dark red like a kidney bean. He whispers something in Bea's ear.

Bea purses her lips. Her eyes get small and hard like the short end of a bullet. "Not if you expect to have another pineapple upside-down cake in your lifetime, buster." Her shoulders swing as she says this.

He whispers again.

Her hands fly to her hips. She glares at him as the wind whips at her scarf.

"Now just you be still and let me do my job here, missus . . ." Darby turns back to us. "Here's how we're going to play this. Boat gets to Alcatraz, you stay put. All of you." He carves a circle with his finger. "Won't have no shenanigans on my watch. Not with the warden on board, you hear? And that goes double for you, missy." He waggles his finger at Theresa.

"Yes, sir." Theresa bounces nervously on her feet as we get closer to where Alcatraz rises out of the water with its layers of green moss and brown residue.

Trixle straightens his hat and ducks back into the cabin as he catches sight of Mae Capone.

I guess she's been to San Francisco before. Otherwise, she'd never wear fur in the summer. Man, it can be cold here when the fog comes in.

"Moose," Annie asks as the gulls suddenly make a ruckus— squawking and complaining like a bunch of old ladies, "if you were to get married, how many kids would you want?" She looks at me seriously.

"How should I know, Annie?"

"Would they all play baseball?"

I shrug. "Why else would you have kids?"

She nods. "Well then. You better make sure your wife can play too. That's my advice to you, Matthew Flanagan," she says.

I roll my eyes. "Whatever you say, Annie," I tell her as we pull into the dock at Alcatraz and the buck sergeant jumps, off winding the rope around the cleat. The cons who take care of the dock and unload the boats are standing at attention as far from the ferry as possible. Quiet as they are in their spanking clean chambray shirts you can feel the excitement run through them like some new kind of electricity has come our way. It isn't every day a woman as beautiful as Mae Capone comes to the island.

The warden gets off first with the Angel Island officers. They walk across the gangplank sure and true as if their legs don't even notice how it dips and rises. Then comes Bea Trixle, taking unsure wobbly steps in her fancy shoes, and three or four people I don't recognize, who must be visiting cons on the island. Officer Trixle is down by the snitch box, which is what we call the metal detector everyone must walk through before entering the island. He is supervising the visitors' walk-through. The next person, a little old lady in a blue hat, triggers the snitch box and it blares. Everybody crowds around to see the show. There's nothing like the snitch box for a little excitement.

The warden motions to Trixle, who trots over to get his orders. Trixle nods and returns to the little old lady. He has her walk back through, triggering the snitch box again. Officer Trixle motions to Bea, who clickety-clacks across the dock, swinging her hips with each step.

"Think it's her corset?" Annie asks. Al Capone's mom visited the island a few months ago and she set off the snitch box with the metal in her corset. Poor woman had to be searched down to her undergarments. She was mortified, never even went up top to visit her son after it happened. She got back on the boat and went home.

"Probably," I say, looking around for Theresa, but she has

disappeared. "Where's Theresa?"

Annie turns around. "Trixle will kill us," she says.

I think again about what Trixle said about Natalie. He makes me so furious I could uproot buildings with my bare hands. Even so, I know my father would not have approved of what I said—or how I said it either. There are so many things to worry about, I can't keep track of them all. I just want this day to end.

"You stay here. I'll find her," I say, but before I can even begin to look, Theresa is back.

"Theresa!" Annie scolds. "You were supposed to stay here."

Theresa's brown eyes are the size of bowling balls. "I saw something," she whispers.

Theresa is always seeing things and imbuing them with great meaning.

"For your book?" Annie asks politely.

"No, Annie. This really happened! Mae Capone dropped her hanky and I saw!" Theresa whispers.

"Yeah, so?" Annie says.

"She didn't pick it up again," Theresa's whisper is throaty. "It was off the boat . . . way off. I'll show you." She pulls on Annie's arm.

"Didn't you hear Trixle? We're supposed to stay put," Annie snaps at Theresa.

"Oh." Theresa's shoulders sink. "It was a pretty one with a hummingbird on it," she says.

"And you could see this from here?" Annie asks.

"I have sharp eyes. My daddy said so."

Bea Trixle is back with the lady in the blue hat. "Earrings," she calls to Darby, jangling a handful of jingling metal.

Darby trots over to the warden and gives this information to him. The warden motions to the woman to come through the snitch box again. This time no alarm. Then comes Mae—I can tell by the sudden buzz of interest from the cons. They aren't the only ones craning their necks to see her either. Half the folks in 64 building are out on the balcony watching.

We're stuck on the boat until Mr. Mattaman comes on board to escort us off. By the time our feet hit the wooden dock planking, the warden, Mae Capone, and Darby Trixle are long gone. Even the cons are back to their sweeping. Theresa skirts around to the spot on the other side of the boat to collect Mae's hummingbird hanky.

It isn't there, of course. We help her hunt for a good twenty minutes, but we don't find anything.

Theresa has her hand on her hips, glaring at us. "You don't believe me, do you?" she says.

"Of course we believe you," I say.

Theresa stamps her foot. "It really happened!"

"We believe you, Theresa," I tell her.

"And you know what else? I touched her! With my hand! When she was talking to Moose. I have so many things to write down. Don't talk to me." She puts her hand over her ears. "I got to go record everything before I forget!"

17. PIXIE GUARD #1

▪▪▪▪▪▪▪▪▪▪▪▪▪▪▪▪▪▪▪▪▪▪▪▪▪▪▪▪▪▪▪▪▪

Tuesday, August 27, 1935

Two laundry days have passed since I gave Mae her yellow rose, and I haven't heard one more thing about it. I'm square with Al now. He's going to leave me alone. My hives are practically gone too; no more wild scratching in the middle of the night. And not even Darby seems to have noticed Mae's yellow rose, burnt up as he was about me giving one to Bea. Thank goodness for Bea and her pineapple upside-down cake, that's all I can say.

Not that I've exactly stopped searching my laundry. I'm like a gold digger the way I check everything: every pocket, every cuff, every sleeve, every pant leg. I pay close attention to the plumbing too because I don't want Seven Fingers coming to my place again. Finding a note in the pocket of my shirt was bad enough. Messing with my pillow . . . that's something else again. A guy's pillow is personal, you know?

Still, all in all I'm feeling pretty good. I don't even mind that school is starting soon, mostly because that means baseball will be beginning too. Annie is going to join us after school. She'll be the only girl, of course. Her mom is pretty proud about this. She's started a new needlepoint pillow to honor the occasion: *Home Run Gal*, it says. So long as she doesn't make one that says *Needlepoint Guy* I guess I'm safe.

Natalie is even doing well. She'll be home for a visit next week. And Scout is coming to the island this afternoon to play ball. I ran this by Jimmy and he seemed fine about it. He said he was glad Scout was coming, so even that little mess has worked out!

This time I decide to run the paperwork for Scout's visit by Darby before turning it in. I'm not taking any chances. I knock on the Trixles' door, but Darby's not there and only Janet is available. "Hi," she says. Her hair is in its usual braids and she has scissors in her hand. "Theresa with you?" she asks hopefully.

"No," I say.

She nods. "Theresa won't play with me. She'd rather play with your sister. And I'm not allowed to play with Natalie. Did Theresa really touch Mae Capone?"

"Yep."

Janet's shoulders sag.

"Nat's not around very much anymore. Maybe Theresa'll play with you now?" I offer.

Janet sighs. "I don't think so. Theresa stays mad a long time."

"Theresa never told me you weren't allowed to play with Nat."

Janet's finger beckons me closer. "She's afraid it will hurt your feelings," she whispers, glancing down at the paper she's cutting. "Hey, look what I'm doing." She perks up. "Making bullhorns. I made a new rule. All my pixie jailers gots to have one."

"Of course. Bullhorns would be essential equipment for pixie jailers."

She nods vigorously, like she's relieved somebody finally appreciates this important concept.

"Would you do me a favor here and look at my paperwork. I've got a friend coming over. I want to make sure it's right."

"Me? You want me to look at it?" She stands up extra straight, puts her scissors down, brushes her skirt off, and tosses her braids behind her shoulders. Then she takes the card.

Normally I wouldn't trust this kind of thing to a seven-year-old, but seeing as how rules are Janet Trixle's specialty . . . Course I don't actually know if she can read. Her finger moves along the page, her lips moving silently, forming the words.

I guess that's my answer. She can read, but not very well. Still, she'll probably tell her dad I consulted her. That can't hurt either.

She nods. "Looks fine. When Scout comes, is Theresa going to play with you?"

"I dunno. Maybe."

Janet's lips are pressed together. She gets her scissors again and resumes cutting. I notice now what's written on the paper bullhorn: *Theresa Pixie Guard #1.*

Thanks to Janet, Scout arrives without a hitch, and Jimmy comes down to the dock to meet him. We're all headed up the switchback to Piper's house to get Annie, when Jimmy suggests a detour through 64. "I've got something to show you, Scout," Jimmy smiles in an un-Jimmy-like way.

"Don't tell me . . . a new species of fly, right?" Scout tries to catch my eye. He clearly thinks this is funny and he wants to share a laugh with me, but I ignore him. I want to be very careful not to hurt Jimmy's feelings.

"No," Jimmy tells him. He leans in to whisper in Scout's ear.

"Really?" Scout answers, craning his neck in my direction, a question in his eyes.

"Yeah." Jimmy's head moves in a bunch of jerky little nods. "I figured you'd want to know."

"Jimmy, where are you going?" I ask as he leads us back around 64 building headed for Chinatown. I grab Jimmy's arm, but he shakes me off. He takes off running to outpace Scout, who is the world's fastest walker. They head down the cement stairway, into the shady cool of Chinatown.

When they get to the secret passageway, Jimmy takes his screwdriver out of his pocket.

"Jimmy!" I groan, but it's too late. He is already unscrewing the hardware that holds the hinge on the door. Jimmy's eyes avoid mine. He opens the door and a cloud of dust swirls into the air. Scout crawls inside.

"Wow," Scout says, his voice dull and distant. "Can you really hear people taking a crap and stuff?"

"Shhh!" Jimmy warns as he climbs in behind Scout.

I don't go in after them. I stand outside fuming. What is Jimmy's problem? How could he tell Scout about this? What kind of a friend is he, anyway?

They stay in there for a long time. I wait, watching Mrs. Caconi's big aprons blow on the clothesline she has back here. She won't let her clothes near the convicts. She washes them all herself.

When they finally come out, Jimmy is apologizing for not being able to play ball with Scout today. The way he does this, it sounds convincing, but I know it's a lie. Jimmy doesn't want

Scout to make fun of him again. That's why he won't play.

"S'okay." Scout brushes the dust from his pants as Jimmy secures the hinges back in place. "Moose was gonna show me this place, right, Moose?" Scout asks.

Jimmy's screwdriver freezes in his hand. He's clearly waiting to hear what I have to say.

But I have nothing to say.

"Sure you were," Jimmy insists, drilling down so hard that his fingers turn white.

Scout's thick eyebrows rise. He looks from Jimmy to me and back again.

"I told Annie about this place too. Seeing as how she's another of your best friends," Jimmy mumbles. "And Piper."

"Piper knows?" I croak.

"Sure. Isn't she your best friend?" Jimmy swings the screwdriver as he walks up the stairs out of Chinatown. Scout and I watch him go.

"He's a good guy," Scout tells me. "You shouldn't make him mad like that."

"I shouldn't? You're the one said he throws like a dead girl."

Scout shrugs as if he doesn't even remember this.

Typical Scout. He's the guy who brings the eggs, but he's never the one with egg on his face. If he wasn't so much fun, I'd hate him.

"Are we gonna play ball or what? Let's go find Annie," Scout suggests, as if playing ball with Annie is the most natural thing in the world.

Annie and Piper are supposed to be singing a song for when J. Edgar Hoover, the head of the FBI, and Eliot Ness, the guy who brought Capone down, come to Alcatraz. Apparently there is going to be a big shindig for them with gold foil invitations and everything.

My mom was supposed to help Annie and Piper practice. She offered to teach Alcatraz kids for half off, but the warden didn't take her up on it. Buddy Boy is helping Annie and Piper with their performance instead.

Buddy Boy's lessons are, of course, free.

When we knock on the warden's door this time, it's Willy One Arm who answers, with the brown mouse, Molly, riding on his shoulder.

"Where's Mrs. Williams?" I ask.

"Not feeling so good," Willy One Arm squeaks. Molly nuzzles his neck, her nose twitching like she's searching for something to eat. We follow Willy and Molly into the living room, where Annie and Piper are both seated on the piano bench.

"Hi, doll." Scout beams his peepers at Piper.

I grind my teeth. Does he have to call her *doll?*

"Hi." Piper smiles back shyly, her eyes softening for Scout.

Piper looks at my baseball bat and her face clouds up. "Annie's busy," she snaps.

Buddy Boy offers me his most inviting smile. "Gonna play a little ball are you, buddy?" he asks, concentrating his magnified gray eyes on me.

"Yeah." I motion my head toward Annie. "When are you gonna be done?"

"She has no idea," Piper answers for Annie.

Scout smiles his old bachelor-guy smile at Piper. "You got a glove, doll? You could play too."

Piper shrugs this off. "You should see this," she tells Scout. "Buddy, do your Shirley Temple."

"Oh now, missy," Buddy says. He can't quite keep the smile off his face. It seems permanently attached to his lips.

"Come on," Piper wheedles.

"Shirley who?" Scout asks.

"You never heard of Shirley Temple?"

Scout shakes his head.

"She's a kid movie star," Annie explains. "They show her movies in the cell house and everywhere else too."

"In the cell house . . . " Scout nods appreciatively.

"Movie night is once a month," Piper explains. "Go ahead, Buddy. You gotta hear this," she tells us.

Buddy clearly lives for this. You can see it in his eyes. He takes off his tortoiseshell glasses and plumps up his curly yellow hair so that it looks more like the six-year-old Shirley's mop head.

Annie rifles through the music until she finds what she's looking for and begins playing.

Buddy Boy walks across the room, swinging his arms at his sides and scrunching his shoulders up like he is an adorable roly-poly mop-headed little girl. His arms soar like an airplane while he sings in a high-pitched voice: "On the good ship *Lollipop*. It's a sweet trip to a candy shop." He rubs his belly and puffs his cheeks out.

If you close your eyes, you'd swear you were listening to Shirley on the radio. Open them and Buddy almost looks like her too. It's a little creepy.

"Look, even Molly likes it." Annie points to Willy One Arm, who is standing in the back, Molly on his shoulder, her keen pink eyes on Buddy while Willy strokes her ratty fur.

I look back at Piper. Scout is right next to her. They are busy whispering to each other.

Buddy catches me watching them. "Moose, you take your friend Scout and run along." He smiles. "We just need a few more minutes, then we'll have your Annie back to you."

Buddy has such a nice way of making me feel comfortable in my own skin. It's as if I'm doing something right every time I see him. He winks at Annie, like they share their own secret.

"He's good, isn't he? Gonna be in vaudeville when he gets out, right, Buddy?" Annie's eyes are bright and completely focused on Buddy.

He can't be a convicted felon. He just can't.

Buddy nods. "You betcha. Got me an agent all lined up. This time next year, you're gonna see my name in lights. Now you go on." He motions to me. "The ladies have more work to do."

Scout and I discuss Buddy as we walk down to the parade grounds. "They let him out to audition?" Scout asks.

"No," I say.

"How'd he get an agent then?"

"Beats me. Hey look here, Scout." He walks so fast I can hardly keep up with him. "Do you have to be so chummy with Piper?"

"Chummy?" He stops on the road, watching a big tanker out in the bay. His eyes are back on me now. "I know a little more about the dolls than you do . . . So, I'm gonna give you some tips." He puts both his hands up in a stop motion. "Don't thank me, okay? It's just what I do for my buddies. But first I need to know . . . you kiss her yet?"

"Shut up, okay?" I tell him. "What makes you think you know so much about girls anyway?"

He rocks his head from side to side like his nose is a pendulum looking for center. "I just do. First thing, don't be going straight for the lips. It's like when you're pitching, you don't want to go straight over home plate but a little to the side to keep 'em guessing. Start with the cheek and then kind of mosey your lips over till . . . bingo!" He taps his lips. "You hit the target.

"Tip two: Watch your nose. Nothin' like a nose smashup to ruin the mood, could even lose you the whole ball of wax. Noses stick out, see, more than lips, so an angle shot is the only way to go." He cocks his head to demonstrate.

Scout holds one finger up. "I'm giving you the best I have here, buddy, I hope you appreciate this." He points to his neck. "Little-known fact. Weak point of every doll in America, a little smackeroo there, you'll have 'em eating out of your hand."

"Look, Scout, let's put it this way." I get my face right up close to his. "You kiss Piper and I don't care if you're my best friend—"

"Hey now, don't get yourself all worked up about *that*. I know Piper's your puppy. But you gotta get a girl warmed up, you know." He points to his chest. "I'm the fella for that job. You betcha."

I sigh, all the resistance drained out of me. "I dunno. She's pretty mad at me. Did you see her?"

"That's because she likes you. That's the way the pretty ones are, Moose. They get mad for all kinds of reasons you can't figure out so don't be wasting your time trying." He taps his finger to his lips. "That's how you solve it right there. Works every time." Scout nods like he's seen this all before.

"Really? You think I should kiss her?"

He sighs as if I'm a sorry specimen of mankind. "What do you think I've been telling you for the last five minutes? Now come on . . . let's go play." He bounces forward down the hill to the parade grounds to wait for Annie, who shows up a few minutes later.

"Piper's sore at you," Annie reports, slipping on her glove.

"She's always sore," I say.

"I mean really sore. She heard about the roses."

"How'd she find out?" I ask.

Annie shrugs. "How's she find out anything?"

"There's no reason for her to be mad about it anyways," I tell her.

Annie knocks on my skull. "Anybody home in there? You're supposed to be her boyfriend, and you didn't even get her a rose."

"Buddy, buddy, buddy." Scout shakes his head. "You didn't get her a rose?"

"I'm not her boyfriend," I insist.

"Yeah well." Annie seems to be enjoying this. "Not now you're not. Jimmy's mad at you too, you know."

"He sure is. Anybody could see that," Scout agrees.

"The trouble is—" Annie's eyes nail me. "You can't stand playing baseball with anyone who isn't as good as you."

"That's not true," I say. "I've never said a word about the way Jimmy plays."

"You don't have to," Annie tells me. "One look at your face says it all."

"It does not."

"Does too."

"I play with you and you're not better than I am." I get right up close to say this.

"Bets?"

"Yeah, bets. Double bets. Triple bets."

"If I were a gambling man," Scout hoots, "I'd put my money on Annie."

"Will you shut up?" I tell him as the sun dips behind a cloud and the parade grounds get dark. The gulls seem to react to this. They begin squawking as if to complain that someone turned the lights off.

There aren't enough players for a real game. So Annie pitches and Scout and I take turns at bat. Every time I get up there I hit so hard, I smack the ball to smithereens. I could take on the Babe today.

"What got into Moose?" Scout asks Annie.

"You just tell him he's lousy," Annie informs Scout, "and he gets like that." She laughs.

"Gonna remember that next time we need a homer," Scout says.

"Yeah," Annie replies, "he's kind of fun that way."

"Shut up, Annie," I say, but now Scout is laughing too. "And stop ganging up on me," I tell them both.

"Poor Humpty Dumpty," Annie says, throwing me one of her best pitches ever, and now I'm so mad I swing the bat so hard I miss.

"Better go easy on him," Scout tells her. "Or he'll fall off the wall."

18. KISSING A DEAD SQUID

■ ■

Same day—Tuesday, August 27, 1935

After Scout leaves, I drop my bat and ball at my house and head for the secret passageway, which I guess needs a new name now that it isn't secret anymore. I'm still mad at Jimmy for telling Scout about this. I don't understand why he did it. Why should I be punished for what Scout said? And the way Jimmy acted, it was like he was sure I'd tell Scout so he decided to do it first. What gave Jimmy the idea I had a big mouth? Just because I'm friends with Scout doesn't mean I'm not Jimmy's friend.

I don't have a screwdriver, but Jimmy didn't put the screws back securely so I jiggle them out with my bare fingers. Inside the dusty space I crawl all the way until I am under Mrs. Caconi's apartment. My plan is to sit here and just think about all of this, but a minute later the door opens and a flash of light flickers at the other end. The door bangs shut. The passageway goes dark again.

Has to be Jimmy. Except Jimmy would never let the door bang. My stomach tightens. The hairs on my arm stand up. Just because there are convicts on this island doesn't mean they'll be under here. The only con that might have access is Seven Fingers.

This does not make me feel better.

It's just Jimmy fooling on me, right? But the steady thumping of hands and knees and a metal clicking are coming my way.

"Jimmy?" I whisper, my voice croaking.

The sound stops. The person doesn't answer and I realize with a start I've just given away my exact location. What an idiot! I scurry off in the opposite direction, when suddenly I see in the half darkness the dark hair and white-ribboned ponytail of Piper.

"Scared you, didn't I?" she whispers, continuing to move toward me. The metal clicking, I see now, is her ring as it hits the ground.

"Of course not," I tell her.

"Liar! Jimmy told me you had to tell the truth in here," she says.

"All right, maybe a little," I admit.

She laughs softly, taunting me. She spits on her fingers, runs them through her hair, pushes a loose strand not held in her ponytail, hooks it behind her ear.

"Don't sit there," I tell her. "Here's better." I pat the dirt next to me. "Not so many ants."

She crawls to where I'm sitting and settles comfortably by me.

"What are you doing in here?" I ask.

"What are *you* doing in here?" She throws the question back at me.

"Just thinking."

"About what?"

"About you," I say.

"You shouldn't think about me. I like Scout now in case you haven't noticed." "I've noticed," I mutter. "I just don't understand why everyone is mad at me."

"I'm the one who should have taken Rocky," she says, our legs barely grazing each other.

"Piper, that was two weeks ago and it wasn't even my fault," I tell her.

"It's only because I'm a girl."

"No, it's because the Mattamans don't trust you."

Piper ignores this. "You guys have it made. You get handed everything on a silver platter. It's disgusting."

"*You're* one to talk."

She snorts. "I wish I was a boy," she admits.

"I don't wish you were a boy. And nobody fawns over me," I tell her.

"Oh yes they do. Mrs. Bomini, Mrs. Mattaman, Theresa, Annie . . ."

"Annie certainly doesn't."

"Are you kidding me? You're all she ever talks about," Piper insists.

"Oh come on." This makes no sense, but I'm not thinking of Annie right now. Piper is sitting so close to me. Her face is perfectly still. I smell her warm root beer breath.

"How come you're not jealous of Scout?" she asks.

"I am jealous of Scout."

This perks her up. "You are?"

Our legs are stretched out in front of us. My calf and hers are barely touching each other, but it feels like a live wire between us. Can she feel it? Or is it just me? It's getting warmer down here. My ears are hot. I'm breathing like I just walked up the switchback. My mind is scrambling.

She *likes me*. She just said she doesn't. But Scout said she did.

I like sitting so close to her. What should I do now? What was it Scout said about going in sideways? I can't just up and kiss her . . . can I? You're not allowed to just kiss a girl, are you? Should I ask her? What if she says no? Why didn't I ask Scout if you're supposed to ask a girl before you kiss her?

Her hand reaches up to my face. She gently brushes my lips, barely touching them.

My head moves toward hers. *How do you avoid nose crashes again? What did Scout say? I can hardly even see her lips it's so dark down here.*

Her hair brushes against my arm. The smell of her baby oil and warm root beer fill my nose. *Are you supposed to have your mouth open or closed?* My teeth nick her lip.

"Ouch!" someone yells.

I jerk my head back.

It takes a second for me to understand that it isn't Piper yelling. It's Theresa looming in the sudden flood of light from the crawlspace doorway. "Moose Flanagan!" Theresa cries. "You stop that right now!"

"You little sneak!" Piper shouts.

Theresa pushes inside. "Am not a sneak. I am *supposed* to find Moose!"

"Get out!" Piper scurries toward Theresa, and Theresa jumps back out of the doorway and grabs the door to keep from falling.

"Moose!" Theresa pleads, hopping around like her leg hurts.

"Go play with someone your own age. Janet Trixle, for goodness' sake. Why do you snoop on me?" Piper shouts.

"I'm not snooping. I had to get Moose." Theresa turns back to me. "Moose, c'mon. Annie needs you."

Piper snorts. "What did I tell you?" she whispers.

"*Annie,* Moose!" Theresa tells me as if this explains everything.

"Hey, look, . ." I'm crawling as fast as I can to the entrance. "Don't do this, okay?" I tell Theresa. "I don't want to be in the middle of this."

"There's nothing to be in the middle of," Piper shouts. She shoves me back and hops out the door. "Just leave me alone."

"Moose!" Theresa stares in at me. "What's the matter with you? You were going to kiss her! I saw!"

"I was not going to kiss her."

"You were! It's sickening! Kissing Piper is like kissing a squid. A dead squid!"

"Not exactly, no."

"No? This isn't the first time! How many times have you kissed her, huh, Moose? How many?" Theresa's hands are on her hips.

"None. I mean . . ." I take a deep breath. "Nothing happened, okay, but look, this is not your business." I crawl out the door.

"Of course it is. *I saved you.* You *owe* me."

"Theresa, you're only seven. When you get older you'll understand."

"I *already* understand. My dad told me all about it. Wildness comes over teenagers like a disease and they go around kissing all over the place. They can't help themselves. If you find yourself about to get smoochy, find Annie or, if you have to, me.

"Oh boy." She sighs, shaking her head and scolding me with her finger. "Wait until I tell Annie."

"Just keep your mouth shut about this, okay, Theresa?"

Theresa nods her head as if I've finally said something that makes sense to her. "I'd be ashamed of myself too. Jeepers, Moose. Jeepers."

19. DRUNK IN THE GUARD TOWER

■■■■■■■■■■■■■■■■■■■■■■■■■■■■■■■■■■■■■

Tuesday, September 3, 1935

Today is my first day in eighth grade. I have Piper in three of my classes but she totally ignores me in school and on the way home too. I'm like a toad squashed flat on the street for all the attention she pays me. She is always a little mad, but this is something different.

Jimmy, Theresa, and Annie don't start school until next week. St. Bridgette's always has less school days than Marina, which isn't fair. Theresa has to go early for orientation and Mrs. Mattaman asked me if I would pick her up after school, so I walk all the way to St. Bridgette's to get her. Theresa is so excited to be in "real school" that she jabbers my head off all the way home.

On the island, we head for the canteen, where we find Jimmy sitting at the counter, his head resting in his hands like he's concentrating on something up close. He doesn't even flinch when the bell on the canteen door rings.

Since what happened with the secret passageway, it has been uncomfortable between Jimmy and me. What isn't said sits like a piece of dog crap between us. I wish it could be the way it was before. Every day I pretend it is and maybe eventually it will be.

"Jim-meeee," Theresa yells, like she always does when he's deep into his projects. "You were wrong. I didn't need my nickel." She waves it in his face. "Ha, ha, I get to get a candy bar."

Jimmy picks his head up slowly, like it's too heavy for his neck. He has a deep crease between his brows.

"Uh-oh," Theresa whispers, "did all your flies die?"

Jimmy has been quite successful with his fly breeding project. Down under the dock he has a big barrel full to the brim with hundreds of flies—maybe more.

"Better go home, Theresa."

Theresa's eyes go wild. "Rocky! Is Rocky. . ."

Jimmy puts his hands up as if to block that idea. "Rocky's okay. It's Dad."

"Dad got hurt?"

"Dad's on probation." He looks at me. "Your dad, too. They got written up for being drunk on guard tower duty."

"What? That's crazy," I say. I'm not even worried about this. That's how nutty it is.

Theresa's mouth drops open, but no sound comes out. Her chin juts forward with the force of this news. "Daddy's never been drunk in his whole life," she declares.

Jimmy shrugs. "Somebody lied, that's all. Somebody's out to get them."

"But why? Why would anyone be out to get Daddy?" Theresa asks as I head out the door and up the stairs as fast as I can.

"Mom." I slam into our apartment. My mom is washing the windows, wearing a pair of my dad's old pants that are too short for her.

She takes one look at me. "You heard."

"Dad wouldn't drink when he's working."

"Of course not."

"Somebody just made this up to get him in trouble?"

"Looks that way. But your dad told me I should simmer down about it. He thinks it was a mistake and it will all get straightened out in due time. I'll tell you one thing. The warden would be a fool to lose your daddy."

"Was it Trixle?"

My mom shakes her head, her lips a cold line. "Darby likes to stir the pot, but I don't think he'd out and out lie."

"Yeah, me either," I agree.

"One thing's for sure. We have to be extra careful until this whole mess works itself out. If you're on probation and you have any trouble, any at all . . . you're gone. No second chances."

"And with Natalie coming home on Friday . . . "

"That's right and that big shindig this weekend too."

"I'll be careful," I assure her.

She takes my chin in her hand. "I know you will be. Six months we lived here with Natalie, we never once had a problem with the warden or Darby either. I suppose I got you to thank for that, Moose." She smiles at me.

I twist my chin gently away from her. My mom doesn't know everything about that time . . . she doesn't know about Nat's friendship with 105, for one thing.

"You know, Moose, Mrs. Mattaman and I were talking. . . ." She pushes the scarf she wears when she cleans away from her eyes. "How are things going with you and the warden's daughter?"

Lately my mom has taken to calling Piper "the warden's daughter." She doesn't refer to her by name anymore.

"You two have a little spat?" my mother asks.

"You could call it that."

My mom folds her cleaning cloth carefully in half and in half again. "You have a little spat, then this thing happens . . . what a coincidence."

"Piper wouldn't do this."

"I hope you're right." The way my mother pronounces *right,* with a hiccup in the middle—ri-ight—tells me she is not convinced.

"She have any reason to be mad at Jimmy or Theresa?" she asks.

"She's mad at Theresa. But Mom, Piper's always mad at someone. That's just the way she is."

"Things are tough at her house right now with a new baby on the way and her momma feeling poorly. You mind your p's and q's around that girl, you hear me? She's pretty as they come, I'll give you that, but she's more trouble than a hornet's nest."

"Yes, ma'am," I say.

"Will you help me empty the pan?" She opens the icebox and takes out the pan filled with melted ice water. Together we walk to the sink, trying to keep the water from splashing.

When we've dumped the water, she takes her rag and gives the pan a good scrub. "Everybody's always telling me how lucky I am to have you. Did you really get Bea Trixle a rose?"

"I guess."

"Did you now?" She directs a smile at her work. "Don't imagine Darby appreciated that any too much."

"I had an extra, that's all."

"A twelve-year-old boy with an extra rose?"

"It's kind of hard to explain, Mom."

"I'll bet it is." She works her cloth into the corner. "Annie's mom says you're interested in needlepoint too?" She looks at me sideways. I roll my eyes.

She smiles her sly smile. "Apparently I'm not giving you the right kind of chores. I wish I'd known. I got some mending needs doing. You interested?"

"Cut it out, Mom," I tell her.

She laughs. "I got a son can do no wrong. Guess I can't complain about that, now can I?"

20. WELKUM HOM NADALEE

■ ■

Friday, September 6, 1935

Nat and my parents are supposed to be on the 4:00 ferry. Theresa, Jimmy, and I are all down waiting for her. Theresa has made a sign. *Welkum hom Nadalee,* it says in pencil with glued-on buttons. My mom got a store-bought lemon cake and I borrowed some of Jimmy's fly harness thread and made Natalie a bracelet.

"Scout be over this weekend?" Jimmy asks as we watch a large fishing boat scoot across the calm water, making a perfect wake, two white lines in the blue .

"Nope."

"You going to Scout's?" Jimmy freezes, waiting for my answer.

"Nope," I say.

Jimmy's head dips down. I don't see him smile, but his dimple is showing, so I know he's happy. "You should see how many flies I have now. Maybe fifty thousand."

"Fifty thousand flies? No kidding?" I ask, scratching my leg, which is driving me crazy. I hope the hives aren't coming back.

Jimmy nods. "They move around so much it's hard to count. Think Natalie could do it."

"If anyone can count fifty thousand flies, it's Natalie."

Jim's brown eyes are full of excitement. "That's what I figured."

"You find out any more about who got our dads on probation?" I ask.

"My mom thinks it's Piper," Jimmy says.

"Everybody thinks it's Piper," Theresa chimes in.

"Piper wouldn't do anything that bad."

Theresa and Jimmy look at each other.

"You got to go talk to her," Jimmy says.

"Why me? You're the one who told her about the secret crawlspace."

Jimmy scoffs. "From what I heard, you didn't seem to mind too much."

I look at Theresa. "You weren't going to tell anyone, remember?"

"Jimmy isn't anyone," Theresa informs me.

Jimmy snorts. "Thanks, Theresa," he says.

"Oh look, Natalie's coming!" Theresa points at the ferry, which is headed toward us, a flock of birds flying above it.

The boat is streaming across the water. The sun is shining through the clouds making the wake sparkle. My dad is handsome in his officer's uniform. My mom is wearing her good green coat. Nat is sitting with her head down like she's reading. From a distance they look so normal.

"Your dad talk to the warden?" Jimmy asks as Mr. Mattaman, who is acting buck sergeant, jumps on the dock. He still has the same duties when he's on probation, they just check on him all the time, like he's a junior officer again.

"I dunno, but he's not worried. He thinks it was only a mistake."

Jimmy shakes his head. "You're just like your dad, you know that?" he snips.

"What's that supposed to mean?" I ask as my father carries Natalie's suitcase with *Natalie Flanagan* written on all sides. He's kidding around with her, pretending to drop her suitcase in the bay. My mother doesn't like this. I can tell by the way her hands are on her hips that she's balling him out.

Natalie says something to my dad that makes him laugh all the more. He hands her back her suitcase. comes up behind us.

Trixle is up in the guard tower. Natalie and my dad come across the gangplank. Natalie is not looking down at her feet like she usually does. She's focused out to the left, her shoulders slumped. She toe-walks across the gangplank and up to the dock. Suddenly the snitch box alarm buzzes loud as an air raid siren.

My mother's back gets stiff as a wheel rod. Her face looks feverish. She stares at Natalie.

Nat's completely quiet—almost like she doesn't hear. She digs her chin in her collarbone.

"Cam," Trixle bellows through the bullhorn from the guard tower. "Mattaman will need to search the suitcase." I know Trixle is itching to do it himself, but he's not allowed to leave the guard tower.

My dad waves to Trixle. "Of course," he says, but when he tries to take Nat's suitcase from her, she won't let go. Probably afraid he'll drop it in the bay.

My mom whispers to her.

"Must have some metal buttons in that button box of hers," my dad tells Mr. Mattaman.

Riv Mattaman smiles kindly. He whispers something in Natalie's other ear. Natalie doesn't look back at him, but I can tell by the angle of her head that she's listening.

When he's finished, her shoulders relax down an inch or two. She hands Mr. Mattaman the suitcase and my mother smiles big enough to cover three or four faces.

I can't help feeling proud of Natalie. First she didn't scream when the snitch box went off and now she hands over her suitcase without a problem. I know she knows her buttons are in there. But still, she lets go.

Mr. Mattaman seems to be explaining something to her. She cocks her head as if she's thinking about this, nods, and then plunks herself down on the wooden dock right where she is. He kneels on one leg, clicks open the suitcase, and he and Natalie lean over to look inside.

Mr. Mattaman puts his hand on Nat's button box. He is clearly asking her if it's okay for him to look inside. My father and Mr. Mattaman are conferring now. Mr. Mattaman nods and holds the button box out to Natalie. Natalie picks out a half dozen buttons and Mr. Mattaman waves the all-clear to Trixle in the guard tower.

"We're all set here, Darby. A handful of metal buttons is all." He leans down to help Natalie buckle her suitcase shut again.

My father rubs his hands together. "All righty then, back in business, Nat."

"Natalie is coming home," Nat says. A tiny smile flashes across her face, bright as a falling star.

"Yes, you are, sweet pea," my dad says. "Yes you are."

21. SHINY BUTTONS

∎∎∎∎∎∎∎∎∎∎∎∎∎∎∎∎∎∎∎∎∎∎∎∎∎∎∎∎∎∎∎∎

Same day—Friday, September 6, 1935

At home Nat wants no part of Mom or Dad. She heads straight for her closet, opens the door, and counts the dresses and blouses hanging there. She skims her hand over the bedcovers. She puts her fingers inside the folds as if she is measuring the depth of each one. She runs her hand, fingers splayed out, along the wall to see if every bump in the plaster is still there. She turns the doorknob and opens and closes, opens and closes the door. She moves on to the bathroom, running her hand along the wall until it hits the towel.

When she's done she comes out to the living room and sits on the couch her hands deep underneath her legs as if she is protecting them. For a second, she looks right at me, which is spooky, like having a teddy bear all your life and one day you see his eyes move. Then she's back to her solid focus on the floor.

"Natalie, it's so nice to have you back," my mom says, her voice choking. But Natalie does not look up. It's as if holding her hands beneath her legs requires all her concentration. "Do you want to unpack your suitcase?"

"Yoo-hoo, Helen! Cam! Yoo-hoo." Mrs. Caconi knocks on the door. "It's your turn."

"Our turn for what?" my mom whispers to my dad.

"Her new icebox. Got one that runs on DC. We have to go see it," my father explains.

"Doesn't she know Nat's here?" my mother asks.

"We have all weekend with Natalie. Moose will keep an eye on her. Mrs. Caconi doesn't have much in her life these days," my dad whispers to my mom.

"Yoo-hoo." Mrs. Caconi is huffing and puffing from her climb up the stairs. "You'll never guess what Bea said."

Mrs. Caconi is standing in our living room. She is big, like her limbs were blown up with a bicycle pump. She has on her good blue flowered apron—the one she wears for entertaining—and her face glows with pride.

"She said she thinks mine is even larger than the warden's. Can you imagine? Of course I didn't get out my measuring tape, but you see what you think."

"Moose, you keep an eye on Natalie while we run down to Mrs. Caconi's. Maybe you and Theresa can help her unpack," my father says before he and my mom follow Mrs. Caconi outside.

Inside Nat's room we watch her go through her buttons, organizing them just how she likes them.

"You're going to go talk to Piper, right?" Jimmy asks.

"I already said I would," I say, trying hard not to sound as annoyed as I feel.

Theresa and Nat sit cross-legged on the floor. Nat unpacks her yellow dress, the special one, which now has seven of Sadie's "good day" buttons sewn neatly in a square on the front.

"Is Mom going to sew buttons on that one when you have a good day here?" I ask. My mom's not much of a seamstress, but she could probably manage a button.

"No Mom. Sadie," Natalie says firmly as she takes out her socks and puts them in her drawer. They make a peculiar thump when she drops them, like they are made of metal.

"You think she'll tell you the truth?" Jimmy is still focused on Piper.

"Hey, wait a minute! What was that?" I jump up and paw through Nat's drawer. My hand snags something hard. I pick up a sock sagging like it's full of stones.

Inside is an enormous metal screw—maybe eight inches long and a good one inch wide with a washer on it.

"What is *that*?" Theresa asks.

"Bottom drawer," Natalie says.

"That was in her suitcase? Let me see." Jimmy takes the big screw from me. He turns the thing over in his hand, twists the washer up, twists it down. "This is for . . . It's used to . . . push things . . . force 'em. . . . apart. Uh-oh!" Jimmy's mouth drops open, like someone poked him hard in the ribs. "I know what this is . . . They use it to push the bars apart. It's a bar spreader," he says.

"What bars?" Theresa asks.

Jimmy leans in to whisper the answer in my ear.

Theresa gives him a swift sock in the arm. "No secrets or I'm telling!"

Jimmy pulls at his glasses. "The prison bars, Theresa, so they can escape," he explains.

Theresa's mouth drops open. "You're lying. That's a big fib, Jimmy Mattaman."

I grab the bar spreader. It's in my hand now. We all stare at it.

"What's it doing in Nat's suitcase?" Theresa asks.

"Nat, how did you get this?" I ask.

Nat doesn't answer.

"That's what set the snitch box off. My father should have found it," Jimmy whispers.

"He thought it was the metal buttons," I say.

"But she's taken her button box through before, it never set the snitch box off. He should have kept looking"—Jimmy again.

"Trixle's not going to like this," I say.

"My dad's already on probation," Jimmy says.

"They're both on probation," I say.

"He'll be fired," Jimmy says in such a low voice I can barely hear him.

"They'll both be fired or . . . or *killed*," Theresa says.

"Not killed, Theresa," I tell her.

"But definitely fired," Jimmy says. "They already think Nat's a security risk."

"We don't have to tell anyone. We can just throw it away, right now," I say.

"Bottom drawer," Natalie mutters, her head twitching left, thend left again.

"Why's she keep saying that?" Theresa whispers.

"How'd you get this, Natalie?"

Nat's hands creep up to her face in that familiar old way. "He told me to."

"Who did? Who is he?"

"105. 105. 105."

"You don't mean Alcatraz 105?" Jimmy whispers.

"105 didn't give you this . . . did he?" My voice cracks high.

Nat's green eyes pass by my face. She cocks her ear to her

shoulder and freezes.

"When did you see 105?"

Natalie dives back in her button box. Stacking and restacking.

"Natalie!"

"Don't yell at her," Theresa barks at me.

"Okay." I blow air out of my mouth and try again as gently as I can. "Nat, when did you see 105?"

Nat is silent.

"We got to get rid of this," Jimmy tells me. "But we can't throw it away. The cons pick up the trash."

"We'll throw it in the bay," I say.

"We can't just take it outside like that," Jimmy says.

"We need a bag." I look around Nat's room for something to wrap around it.

Natalie's grip is tight on the bar spreader. "Bottom drawer. Bottom drawer, bottom." She begins to spin in her spot.

"Natalie." I put my hand out to steady her, but she's spinning even faster now. "He said to put it in the bottom drawer." She struggles to say the sentence correctly, struggles to be understood, as if that is the only problem here.

I try to make my voice as calm as possible. "That's good, Natalie. That's just right. But I need it, okay? Will you let me borrow it?"

"No," she says, each time she comes around, "no, no, no." She spins faster and faster.

The door bangs. My parents are back. I hear them in the living room. "How much do you think it put her back?" my dad asks my mom.

Natalie has her hand on the bar spreader. She won't let go.

"We should tell," Theresa says.

"My dad will tell the warden. And he'll be fired," I say.

"They won't be fired if we tell the truth." Theresa is firm about this.

"Sure they will, Theresa. They messed up," Jimmy explains.

"Natalie," I say. She's still spinning but not so fast. "Look, I'll give you five buttons for this, okay?"

She stops. Her eyes get suddenly bright. "Five gold buttons?"

I know the ones she means. They're on my suit jacket—the one I wear for special occasions. She loves those shiny gold buttons. My mom will kill me if I cut them off, but what else am I going to do?

"The gold ones you like," I tell her, trying to wiggle the bar spreader out of her grasp.

She nods, but doesn't let go.

I get the scissors and my good suit jacket and snip off the gold buttons, while she plays with the bar spreader, absorbed in twisting the little screw and washer up and down.

"Here. Five gold buttons." I toss the buttons in my hand. They make a satisfying clinking sound.

Nat seems not to hear. All her attention is on the bar spreader.

"It's nice she's got something she's proud about. It must be so hard for her on her own." My mom's voice from the other room. Then she stops. "Moose, awful quiet in there. Everything okay?" she calls through the door.

"Yeah, fine." I try to make my voice sound normal.

"Nat," I whisper. "Let's take the bar spreader with us, okay? Let's put it in this bag." I grab my tote and offer it to her. "You can carry it."

Nat takes the bar spreader and carefully places it inside. Then she holds the bag close to her, the way my gram holds her pocketbook when she thinks pickpockets are around. I motion to Nat, Jimmy, and Theresa to follow me.

"Dad, we're going out," I tell him as he walks into the kitchen and pours himself some coffee.

"Not now, Moose." His voice cuts a crisp line.

"We're taking Natalie with us," I say.

My father shakes his head. "It's getting late. I want you to stick around here today."

"Bottom drawer," Natalie says, carrying the tote bag back to her room.

"Sounds like she hasn't finished unpacking yet," my father points out.

"Okay sure," I say awkwardly, and then hurry Natalie back in her room before she says anything else.

Once I get the door safely closed behind us, Jimmy and I stare at each other. "What are you going to do now?" he asks.

"I'll think of something," I whisper.

"What?" Theresa wants to know.

"I haven't thought of it yet."

Theresa nods, but she's screwed up her face.

"Natalie." It suddenly occurs to me. "You want to give Theresa the bar spreader. She gave you those checkers, remember? You need to give her something back."

Natalie appears to be thinking about this. She rocks back and forth. "Hair comb," she decides.

"Theresa already has a hair comb. She wants that bar spreader. You want Theresa to be your friend, don't you?"

"Friend." Nat keeps rocking, holding the bar spreader tight to her chest. "Friend, friend, friend."

Uh-oh. I don't like the way she's doing this. What if she throws a tantrum with the bar spreader in her hands? How in the world will I explain that?

"Nat, please don't pitch a fit. *Please*," I beg.

"It's okay, Moose." Theresa pats my arm like she is twelve and I am seven. "She's just talking . . . aren't you, Nat?"

"Friend, friend, friend," Nat says, but I see her arms slowly unfurl from her chest, then her hands and fingers.

Theresa waits quietly until Nat gives her the bar spreader. "Thank you, Natalie," she says.

"Throw it in the bay," I whisper in Jimmy's ear. "Get it out of here for good." Jimmy nods, his eyes keen.

"I know! I can handle it, Moose, okay?" Jimmy snaps.

"Sure," I whisper. "Of course."

When he's gone I feel better for about thirty seconds and then I begin to understand the full extent of the problem.

Somebody expects to find a bar spreader in her bottom drawer. Somebody will be looking for it very soon.

22. TOILET'S STOPPED UP

■ ■

Saturday, September 7, 1935

The next day when I get up, the sun is shining brightly on the sparkling blue water. I watch the birds fly by our front window. A gull skims low on the water. A cormorant flies by fast like he's late. A pelican dips and soars like a stunt plane.

Things aren't so bad, are they? I need to relax, I decide as I head for the bathroom.

"John's a little sensitive. Don't use too much toilet paper," my father calls out from the kitchen.

The door to the bathroom is open. A chocolate bar sits on the sink.

I try to keep my voice steady. "Seven Fingers is coming?"

"You betcha. He's on his way right now. Your mom's gonna take Nat out to the swings so she won't be underfoot."

"Why? We weren't having plumbing problems last night." I try to keep the panic out of my voice.

"We're always having plumbing problems," my dad says.

My mom is watching me. Her eyes are full of concern. "You worried about Trixle?"

"Yeah," I say, though right now Trixle is the least of my worries.

"Don't blame you. I can't stand the guy," my mom mutters.

"C'mon, Nat, let's get out of here."

"But Dad," I say when they're gone. "I don't understand this. The toilet is working fine."

He shrugs. "Pipes are all hooked together, Moose. One person's having plumbing troubles and we all are. The whole building needs to be replumbed."

"Sure," I agree, "but why today?"

My father gives me a puzzled look. "Why not today?" he asks as the sound of footsteps approaches.

My father looks out on the balcony. "Darby." He heads for the door, props it open for Trixle and Seven Fingers.

Trixle walks in, hitching up his trousers. Right behind Trixle is skinny, creepy Seven Fingers with his shaved knob of a head. I look down at his hands. Two fingers are missing from his left hand. On his right hand there is a stump like a notch where his index finger should be.

"Come on in, Darby." My father moves out of the way so they can come in. Seven Fingers is the picture of obedience, following along behind Darby. Seven Fingers's eyes never leave the carpet, but it seems like he sees everything, sucks it all in without looking up.

My father touches his officer's cap to greet Seven Fingers. Seven Fingers nods, without meeting my father's eyes. Darby curls his lip at my father. He and my father don't agree about anything. Even the way my father says hello to the cons is a problem for Trixle. Too respectful. Trixle would have every convict on a leash like a dog if he could.

"All right, then, have a look, see what you think." My father waves toward the bathroom.

Seven Fingers goes into the bathroom, Trixle stands outside, leaning against the wall, first one way, then the other. He shifts his feet, eyeing our living room sofa. He seems to decide that Seven Fingers will be all right, marches into the front room, and plunks himself down.

"Can I get you something, Darby?" my father asks.

"Don't happen to have any of Anna Maria's cannolis around, do you?" Trixle asks, putting his shiny black shoes on the coffee table. "Ain't nobody can make 'em the way she can."

My father nods toward me. "Moose, could you run to the Mattamans' and ask Anna Maria if she can spare a cannoli?"

When I get back with cannolis for Trixle on one of Mrs. Mattaman's yellow flowered plates, Seven Fingers is in the living room. "Trouble's worse than I thought. Them army pipes are three-quarter inch," Seven Fingers says in a whispery tobacco voice. "They get jammered up real easy. Got some 'bout ready to burst. Need to replumb the whole dang place, sir."

Trixle grunts. "Not going to replumb the whole dang place, that's for sure. Get the ones 'bout to burst, then we'll call it a day."

Seven Fingers cocks his head like his hearing is bad. His eyes are on the cannolis.

"You heard me. Get a move on," Trixle growls, Seven Fingers sidles back to the bathroom.

I stay on the couch until Trixle and my dad get to talking about politics.

My dad's eyes are riveted on Trixle. "WPA's gonna get the whole country working again," he insists.

"Ain't nothing but handouts," Trixle shoots back.

"Can't say I agree with you on that." My father grinds his

teeth.

This is my chance. I have to take it. But my legs feel like they are mortared to the couch cushion and my hands are wet with sweat.

"I understand you got yourself a problem with your little girl, Cam. But this ain't about that."

"Doesn't have anything to do with Natalie, Darby."

"I'm only saying your situation's one thing and the WPA is another."

I've made my legs move. They are walking down the hall with me inside them. Trixle and my dad don't seem to notice. My heart is beating so hard it feels like little explosions in my chest.

Seven Fingers has the bathroom door half closed and the water running.

A towel is slung across the knob. "Seven Fingers?" I whisper. My mouth is so dry I can hardly get the words out.

I peek in, but Seven Fingers isn't in the bathroom. I take a deep breath, turn, and push open the door to Natalie's room.

The bottom drawer is open. The shadow of Seven Fingers stands behind the door. His tall thin chest slips past me and back into the bathroom.

My heart pounds in my ears. My arms are stiff as sticks of wood. "You stay away from her," I say.

"This ain't kid stuff," he murmurs, the smell of bad breath and tobacco filling my nostrils. "We know where she sleeps." The bathroom door shuts almost silently in my face.

23. SEVEN FINGERS'S CANDY BARS

▪▪▪

Same day—Saturday, September 7, 1935

"We need to talk," I tell my dad when Seven Fingers has gone.

"Can it wait until tomorrow?"

"No."

A darkness falls across my father's face. He slips his toothpick box into his pocket and motions with his head toward the door. "How about we go for a walk? Could use a little fresh air," he says.

We tromp down the stairs to the dock and around the agave trail, which runs low along the water. The wind blows hard, as it often does late in the day. It feels like a giant hand pushing us back. But my father is determined. He's headed for a spot on the hillside looking out across at San Francisco. We sit down on rocks jutting out of the hill.

I look into his kind golden brown eyes. "Dad, what if the Esther P. Marinoff School isn't as safe as we thought?"

"What do you mean safe?"

"What if . . ." I work at a stone with my heel, try to loosen it from the dirt. "What if Natalie isn't safe there?"

His eyes squint with the effort to understand. "Safe you mean how?"

"What if she was getting visitors?"

"Visitors? For crying out loud, Moose. What are you driving at?"

The rock comes free. I hold it in my hand. "I'm worried about the convict 105."

"105?" my father says as a gust of wind blows his officer's cap off.

"The gardener. He worked over here. Piper said he got released from Terminal Island a few weeks ago."

"Oh yes, Onion. Why in the Sam Hill are you worried about him?"

"Because . . ." My voice trails off. I'm about to tell him how Seven Fingers said he knew where she slept. On the island? At the Esther P. Marinoff? Which is worse? I don't even know.

"Because?" my father prompts.

"I dunno, I just—what if 105 visited Natalie at school?"

My father stares at me. "What on earth makes you think he'd do that?"

"I had a . . . a dream. A nightmare."

He breathes out a huge gush of air. "For Pete's sake, Moose. You had me goin' there for a minute."

"Could he find her?" I ask.

"Why would he want to, son? She doesn't have money. We don't have money. They could kidnap her, I suppose, but it wouldn't be worth their while. She's safer there than she is almost anywhere."

"What about here then?"

"Moose, look at me." He waits until my eyes connect with his. "I'd never bring my family on this island if I thought there was any real danger. That cell house is sealed up tight as a drum. Try to stop worrying so much. Ollie thinks your nerves could be triggering the hives."

I find a smooth rock and sail it into the bay. "I don't trust Seven Fingers."

"Good! I wouldn't want you to trust him."

I find another rock and throw it as hard as I can. "I don't want him in our apartment."

My father nods. "Don't much like him here myself. I wish those city plumbers didn't cost an arm and a leg . . . But you know what? Our plumbing problems never seem to get that much better. It's occurred to me that old Seven Fingers likes his chocolate bars a little too much." He fishes in his pocket for a new toothpick.

Sometimes it feels like our life is made out of toothpicks and if I pull one out, the whole thing will collapse.

"I like the way you're thinking all of this through. Sometimes life throws you a punch and you just have to reason it out for your own self. You can't always accept what other people tell you.

"Once when Natalie was little, a doctor told us what she had was contagious. If we kept her at home with us, you could catch it from her. He said we should send her away to a ranch in Arizona where she would be quarantined so as not to infect others.

"You were so healthy. Everything I ever wanted in a son." He sighs and presses his lips tight together. "I couldn't risk you getting this terrible thing she has, this blackness that eats her up from the inside. But I couldn't ship my daughter off like she was no more than livestock. I went around and around trying to reason it out, but in my gut I knew the answer. I wasn't going to send Natalie off like that. If she were infectious, wouldn't we have caught it already? The next week we went to another doctor who said there was no evidence her condition was contagious. None at all.

"You got a good noggin." He knocks on my head with his fist. "I'm not worried about you."

"And Natalie?" I whisper. "You worried about her?"

He looks out across the bay to San Francisco. The streets are so straight and orderly over there. Everything makes sense in the city.

"Her life isn't gonna go the expected way. But just because she doesn't see the world like you and me doesn't mean she isn't getting just as much out of her days as we do. Who are we to say what life's supposed to be about, Moose? Who are we to say that?"

24. A DEAL WITH THE WARDEN'S DAUGHTER

. . . .

Same day—Saturday, September 7, 1935

First things first. I have to get my dad and Mr. Mattaman off probation. Then if something happens, they won't automatically be fired. This means I need to talk to Piper. I still don't think she's the culprit, but everybody else is sure she is.

I consider taking Jimmy to Piper's, but I decide against it. It will be better if she doesn't feel we're ganging up on her.

Okay, there's another reason too. It has to do with how her ears poke out of her hair and the softness of her skin—like a brand-new baseball, only better.

I'm on my way up to the warden's house, a warm wind blowing my hair back out of my face and making it twice as hard to walk uphill, when my mom waves me down. She has her hat and her gloves on, and her music satchel is tucked under her arm. "We've been looking all over for you, Moose," she says. "Could you keep an eye on Natalie for a few hours? I just got a call from a family in the city. They want me to interview this afternoon . . . four private lessons at full freight . . . now that's good money."

"Now? I was just headed for Piper's house."

My mom's face clouds. "I need to get a move on," she says. "I have to give myself time to find the place."

"Could I take Natalie along?" I don't look directly at my mom when I ask this. I'm afraid of what she'll say.

"To the warden's house?" My mother's voice is incredulous.

"She's been there before with me," I wheedle.

"Yeah, but with Mrs. Williams feeling so poorly, I don't think it's a good time. And you know Daddy's still on probation, Moose."

I'm itching to tell her that's exactly why I need to go up there. I want her to know this isn't kid stuff. "Mom, it's important."

She takes a deep breath and asks. "Why?"

I think about telling her exactly why I need to go up there. I want her to know this isn't kid stuff, but I'm afraid she'll say this is Daddy's business, not mine.

"Mom, it's important."

She takes a deep breath and asks, "why?"

"What if Dad says it's okay?" This is a gamble. Sometimes it makes my mom mad when I suggest consulting with my dad, as if her opinion isn't enough.

"Let's see what he has to say," she answers, hurrying on her high heels to the electric shop.

So far so good, I think as she pokes her head in the electric shop door. "Cam!" she says. "I have a chance at four new privates but I need to go in and interview this afternoon. What do you think about Moose taking Natalie up to the warden's house?"

My father is up on a stepladder, pulling down a wooden soda pop crate where he keeps nails and screws and bolts organized by size. He fishes his hand in one of the squares. "What business do you have up there? And how long will it take?"

"I have to talk to Piper and it won't take long. An hour maybe."

"You'll keep a close eye on your sister?"

"Of course."

"You can handle this, right, Moose?" He jingles wing nuts in his hand.

"I can handle it," I tell him.

My father nods to my mother but doesn't meet her eyes. "We can't keep her locked up in the house all week, Helen."

My mom's bottom lip puckers out.

"Sadie will read us the riot act if we don't let her go with the other kids," my dad continues. "You know that as well as I do."

My mother nods a small unwilling okay to me. She watches me and Nat walk up the switchback. I know she's worried about Natalie, like always, but there's something else in her eyes— something I'm not used to seeing She's worried about me too.

In the distance, the boarding whistle blows and the buck sergeant hollers last call. I hear the clickety-click of her high heels as she runs down to the dock, clutching her music bag in one hand and keeping her hat on her head with the other.

Natalie walks along at her own pace oblivious to the gusty wind that picks up a leaf and blows it against her cheek. She operates out of her own cocoon, which she takes with her wherever she goes. She doesn't follow me, lead me, or walk by my side but seems to drift along like we are caught in the same gust of wind. I explain we'll be visiting Piper. I tell her if she's good, I will bake her a lemon cake.

She appears to be ignoring me, but then I hear her say almost to herself, "No bake."

I laugh. Natalie knows I can't cook. I once tried to bake her alphabet cookies and they were so hard you could shoe horses with them.

When we get to the warden's mansion I ring the bell several times before Willy One Arm opens the door with Molly on his shoulder. "It's Moose," he calls out.

Nat looks up from her shoes, directly at the mouse. "Mouse," she whispers, her voice loaded with excitement.

"Let him in." I hear Buddy's voice in the background. Willy One Arm scoots out of the way. Buddy and Piper are playing checkers in the living room. From the number of glasses, empty plates, and crumpled napkins on the table, it looks like a marathon tournament. Piper is studying the board. So many wisps of hair have come free from her ponytail that there can't be much back there anymore. It looks as if she slept in her clothes.

Right now, the island is being scrubbed and shined from one end to the other in preparation for the visit of the head of the FBI. Just this morning I heard the warden chewing out Associate Warden Chudley because the whitewall tires on the Black Mariah weren't brand spanking clean and there were dead plants in the flower beds. So why would the warden's own house be in such disarray?

Willy One Arm walks back to his seat at the dining room table, where he has a long list of numbers in front of him. His hands are busy shining a pair of shoes—probably the warden's—while his eyes scan the list of numbers.

"Mouse," Natalie mutters, her eyes on Molly, who sits on One Arm's shoulder as if she's supervising his work. I position myself between the two rooms so that I can see both Natalie and Piper.

I know Piper sees me here, but she ignores me.

"Could we talk?" I ask her as the sound of a bell tinkles from the kitchen.

Buddy Boy shoves his feet in his shoes. He fishes his tie out of his shirt pocket and tosses it over his head, shimmying the knot up beneath his Adam's apple as he heads for the kitchen.

Piper watches him, a hollow look in her eyes. "Go away," she says.

"Really, Piper. We have to talk," I tell her.

She glares at me. "No, we don't."

I walk over and sit down on a nearby chair, then scoot it over so I can still see Natalie. She and the mouse are transfixed as if they have just discovered something significant in common.

Piper pushes the wisps of hair out of her face with the heel of her hand. Her foot fidgets, and she glances up in the direction of the bell.

"Come on, Piper. Please. This is important," I tell her as Natalie reaches her hand out to Molly, who scampers onto her palm. Willy One Arm looks up from his page. His hand hovers over the mouse, as if he's ready for her back, but Natalie has her face right up close to Molly, whispering urgently to her.

"Give the mouse to Willy," I tell Natalie.

"Her name is Molly," Nat mutters.

"Give Molly back," I say, turning my attention toward Piper.

Piper continues to study the checkerboard as if it is endlessly interesting. "Please, can we talk outside?" I ask.

"What do you want to talk about?"

"It's private." I motion with my thumb to the door.

"I'm busy," she says, but her voice is thick as if she has a cold.

"When will you be free?" I ask as Buddy Boy comes back from the kitchen.

"Is Mommy okay?" Piper asks in a small voice.

"She is." Buddy smiles warmly at her. "Don't you worry, Piper my girl. She's just fine."

Piper seems to take this in. It perks her up considerably.

I try again to catch her eye, but she ignores me. She's clearly not in any mood to talk today, plus it feels creepy in this house and I want to be out of here.

"Let's go, Natalie. Give Molly back," I tell her.

Natalie is petting the mouse with one finger, across her head and down her back, across her head and down her back, each time the exact same route.

"Natalie, please," I wheedle.

But every fiber of Natalie's being is focused on petting Molly.

Willy One Arm looks up from his numbers, slips his hand around the mouse, and slides her into his shirt pocket in one greased motion.

Uh-oh. I'm not sure how Nat's going to take this. Once she smacked a guy who messed with her buttons—punched him right in the kisser. The guy wasn't hurt, but my mother was mortified. She gave the man twenty whole dollars on the spot and begged him not to press charges.

"C'mon, Natalie," I plead, wishing I could grab her and carry her out of there. "We can see Molly tomorrow."

"Tomorrow. We can see Molly tomorrow," Nat mutters.

"That's right, Natalie," I say.

And then as if a circuit switch flips inside Natalie's brain, her face relaxes, her shoulders ease down to where they're supposed to go, and she trails after me.

I open the front door and we troop out, but before I get the door closed, Piper slips outside with us.

"I thought you wanted to talk," Piper asks innocently, as if I were the one refusing.

"I do," I tell her as I sit on the steps. Piper leans against the house and Natalie rocks on one foot, as if this motion is endlessly interesting.

I take a deep breath. "I don't know how to say this . . . but did you have anything to do with getting my dad and Mr. Mattaman on probation?"

Piper scratches her ear. "Who wants to know?"

"I want to know."

Piper stares at the cell house, a blank look on her face. "Maybe."

"Maybe? You either did or you didn't, Piper."

I wait for her to answer. She continues to watch the cell house.

"I told everyone you wouldn't lie like that," I tell her, my voice full of acid.

Even as I say this I know how ridiculous it is to tell her this. Piper always lies to get her way. Everyone lets her too. If my mom and Mrs. Mattaman thought Piper was responsible for getting my dad and Mr. Mattaman put on probation for no reason, why didn't they call her on it? Because she's the warden's daughter. That's why.

"You were wrong. Theresa deserved it and so did you. You didn't stand up for me. You were just worried about making Theresa mad." She snorts. "Nobody can ever be mad at poor little Moosey. You have to make sure everybody loves you every stupid minute."

"I don't like to collect enemies the way you do, if that's what you mean."

She shrugs. "Oh, who cares anyway. This is boring."

"It's boring? You get my dad and Mr. Mattaman on probation for nothing and then you say it's boring?"

"So what do you want me to do about it?"

"Tell the truth."

She rolls her eyes. "Why would I do that?" she asks like she really doesn't know.

"Because it's the right thing to do."

"You actually think that matters to me?"

I've never met anyone as irritating as Piper. She makes me feel like I've got gun powder exploding in my veins.

"I'll tell you what," she suggests. "I'll get this squared away, but then you'll owe me."

"You mean you'll tell your dad the truth?"

"Of course not. I'll tell him that I thought it was booze they were drinking. It was clear and gold like beer, but it was only apple juice."

"How will you explain not telling him this before?"

Her green eyes are clear and keen. "I felt so awful about what happened." She makes her voice tremble with emotion. "I couldn't bring myself to tell you." She dabs at her eyes.

What a performance! How can I like this girl? I make myself sick.

But even now I'm watching her lips, the curve of her arms, the shine of her hair. Messy as she is today, she's still beautiful.

"But like I said," she continues, "you'll owe me."

"I'll owe you what?"

"I haven't decided yet." She takes a step closer, leans down so she's right in my face. I breathe in the sweet talcum smell of her. Her lips brush my cheek and everything inside me hits a pothole.

"Piper, can I ask you something?" I whisper. "Couldn't you be just a little nicer?"

"Now?" She strokes my cheek, ever so gently, just where her lips touched it. The sweet powerful smell of her comes over me like a hot sweat.

"No," I tell her as I reach my hand out to hold her chin, gently, so gently. "All the rest of the time?" I whisper as my lips find her lips. I don't know if this is the way you're supposed to do this, but suddenly I don't care about Scout and his instructions. I'm going to do this my way.

"Theresa," Natalie whispers, startling me. I'd forgotten all about Natalie, but here she is, swaying back and forth between her two feet as if she's on a rocking horse. And then I see Theresa and Jimmy running up the hill toward us and I can feel the deep flush of blood in my face, but my back is to them. I don't think they saw.

Still, I can't believe it's Theresa *again*. That girl has a knack for being where she's not supposed to be.

"Moose," Jimmy calls. "We need you!"

"Moose, we need you," Piper mimics, her voice sour. She glares at me, turns, and walks back into her house, the door closing hard after her.

"Moose kiss," Nat mutters. "Moose is kissing."

My face gets so hot I feel like I just stuck my head in the oven, but Jimmy and Theresa are so upset they don't hear Natalie.

"Just tell him, Jimmy," Theresa prods.

"Shut up, Theresa," Jimmy says, his cheeks flushed. He straightens his glasses one way, then straightens them the other, as if he can't find plumb on his nose.

"Tell me what?"

Jimmy kicks the ground. "I messed up," he mutters, his face scarlet, "I threw it, okay? I did, but—"

"Threw what?"

"The bar spreader. Janet Trixle has it," Theresa blurts. "She's using it in her carousel. All of the painted ponies are tied to it. And she has a hot pad on the top for the tent cover."

"How'd she get it?"

"Must have washed back up on the beach and she collected it in her beach bag. Took it home and used it for her carousel." Jimmy still can't look at me.

"She doesn't know what it is?"

Jimmy and Theresa both shake their heads.

"But Darby knows what it is . . . We are in so much trouble," I say.

"She's got it decorated like a barber pole," Jimmy explains.

"It's right in front of his nose and he hasn't noticed yet?"

"Hiding in plain sight," Jimmy whispers.

"That's the best way to hide something. That's what my dad says. C'mon, we gotta get it out of there."

"Darn straight we do," Jimmy agrees.

"Natalie!" I shout. "Let's go!"

25. THE BAD GUYS ARE LOCKED UP

··

Saturday, September 7, and Sunday, September 8, 1935

Natalie shuffles along faster than usual. Just watching her come down the switchback, doing her best to keep up, fills me with a rush of gratitude. She is trying in her own weird way. She really is.

I wonder what she'll make of the kiss. Of course, the one moment I wish she'd been lost in her own world, she wasn't. But it wasn't like she stood there and stared or anything. Piper didn't even mention her and she would have if Natalie had been staring.

All of this is rushing through my mind as we head for the Trixles'. It's not until we have arrived pell-mell at the door of the largest apartment in 64 building that it occurs to me we need some reason to be here.

"You're visiting Janet," I tell Theresa as I knock on the door.

"Me? Why me?" Theresa scowls.

"C'mon, Theresa," Jimmy wheedles. "You can be nice to her for five minutes. We have to get the bar spreader back."

"How am I supposed to do that?" Theresa's hands are on her hips. "She's not going to just hand it over to me, you know."

I knock again. Still no answer.

Theresa looks at me, her lips pressed so hard together her chin wrinkles. "You can't take Natalie inside," she whispers.

"Why not?"

"Because," Theresa mutters. She looks to Jimmy for help.

"They're not home anyway," Jimmy declares.

"Shall we go in?" Theresa asks, frowning.

Jimmy and I look at each other.

"We can't just take it. Wouldn't that be stealing?" Theresa wants to know.

I wiggle the knob. "It's locked anyway."

Doors are never locked on Alcatraz. Our parents say it's safer here than in San Francisco because all our bad guys are locked up. We are used to running in and out of each other's houses.

Of course, we don't run in and out of Darby Trixle's house, so we never noticed his door is locked.

"What do we do now?" Jimmy asks.

"Wait for them to get home," I reply.

"She found it on the beach, though," Jimmy reasons. "Why is that our fault? No one has to know how it got there."

"Yeah, but it's dangerous. If Seven Fingers were to get his hands on it . . ." I explain.

"Go ahead and say it," Jimmy growls. "It's because I throw like crap. This would never have happened if Scout had thrown it."

"Scout would have wanted to keep it as a souvenir or else he'd trade it," I tell him as we walk back down the stairs to our apartments.

"That's not what you really think," Jimmy grumbles.

"Am I mad about this, Jimmy? Do I look mad?" I ask, though

I can feel as I say this that I'm beginning to get angry.

"You are, though."

"What do you want me to say here? Just tell me so I'll know," I ask him.

"Why don't you just tell the truth for a change?"

"What are you talking about? I always tell you the truth."

"No, you don't. You tell me what you think I want to hear, same as you tell everyone else."

I open my hands as if to show him I'm not holding anything inside. "I'm not mad, okay, Jim?"

"You are, though. You're mad because I messed up and you're embarrassed that I can't play ball."

"Look, I'm not embarrassed. But yeah, I do wish you liked baseball. What's the matter with that?"

Jimmy whistles long and low. "I thought you were different. You're just like everyone else." He turns on his heel and walks back to his apartment.

Theresa is silent. Her mouth hangs open. Her dark eyes are big as goggles. "Jimmy doesn't get mad at anyone but me, not ever," she says.

All through the evening, I check on the Trixles, but they don't come home. By nightfall, I know I'll have to wait until tomorrow. I just can't think of a reason I'd need to see them that late at night. Not one that wouldn't make Trixle suspicious anyway. First thing tomorrow I'll deal with it. I'll go in and talk to Janet. Tell her Jimmy is going to make her a much better carousel. He wants to take hers and use it as a model. Then when we get it to the Mattamans' we'll switch out the bar spreader and get rid of it for good.

■ ■ ■

In the morning when I get up, the trim on 64 building is being painted, the extra dock equipment is being hauled out of sight, the steps to 64 are swept, the windows washed, the roof of the dock tower is being scrubbed, the bird turd removed. The *Coxe* has a new coat of paint, the brass fixtures shined bright as Natalie's favorite buttons, and there are convicts washing the road.

I find Bea at the canteen stacking cans of tomato sauce in a perfect pyramid. "Where's Janet?" I ask.

"We took her down to Monterey to visit her cousins. They have a horse," Bea tells me, as if this explains everything. But that's all I get out of her. Bea is in no mood to chat. She was gone yesterday and the deliveries have backed up. She needs to get the new groceries out, she tells me, plus there's the party preparation and hairstyling to do. It seems suddenly as if the visit of Hoover and Ness has commandeered all the adults' attention.

In the afternoon, on the way back from getting their hair done at Bea Trixle's, Piper and Annie knock on my door. "We need to talk," Annie says. Her hair looks odd, as if it has been curled and pinned into a position entirely against its wishes. Even in her baseball pants, Annie does not look comfortable. Piper's hair is styled the same way, but on her, it looks glamorous.

We go back in my room and close the door. It feels awkward and small in here and stinky with the goop Bea Trixle put on their hair.

Annie sits on a crate, Piper sits on my bed, and I stand up, not sure what to do with myself.

"I'm going to the party," Piper informs me.

"Of course you're going. You're performing," I say.

"Yeah, then I'm supposed to leave, but I'm not going to. I want to see Scarface." Piper seems more like her usual self today. That's good, I guess, but it's also bad.

"And you're going to stay with me," she points at me like she's shooting me with her finger.

"No, I'm not."

"You owe me and *you know why.*" Her finger takes deadly aim.

"Why?" Annie wants to know.

"I can't stay with you. I have to watch Natalie," I tell her.

Piper smiles. "Already taken care of. Mrs. Caconi is going to do it."

"My parents won't agree to that," I tell her.

"They already have." Piper gloats. "My dad asked them. They can't turn my dad down."

"Wait a minute. You told your dad you want to meet Scarface and he agreed?"

"No, stupid. I told him I wanted you to see our performance."

"What's that have to do with Scarface?"

"Nothing so far as he knows. We'll hide, then we can watch. Capone is supposed to be the waiter. And he'll put on a show. That's what Buddy said."

"I'm not getting in trouble. My dad's on probation." I glare at her. "We'd be kicked off the island if I were caught."

"Then our deal is off."

"You're heartless, you know that?" I tell Piper.

"What deal?" Annie insists.

"None of your business," Piper snaps, scratching at her hair. "Look." She turns to me. "If I'd been a boy my dad would have let me sit at the table. You can bet that."

"What's that have to do with anything?" I ask.

"You don't know anything." She snorts. "Look, you might as well give up. I got your dad on probation, I can get him fired too."

Annie's mouth drops open.

"Guess Annie knows now," I tell Piper.

"Yeah, so . . . what do you say?" Piper turns to her.

"You got to do what she wants. You don't have a choice," Annie answers in a gentle voice that seems as unlike her as her hairdo does.

Piper smiles triumphantly. "Did you hear that, Moose? Even Annie agrees with me."

26. AL CAPONE IS THE WAITER

....

Sunday, September 8, 1935

The warden is out this morning making sure everything looks just so. He had the Black Mariah polished up shiny as patent leather. It's sitting ready to drive J. Edgar Hoover and Eliot Ness up the hill to tour the place. The dock itself was scoured, the underside scrubbed with bristle brushes. The stink of moss and rotting algae has been replaced with the good smell of clean laundry and Ivory Soap. You'd think Hoover and Ness were royalty, the way the warden is acting.

My dad spends half an hour polishing the badge on his hat with special cream my mother bought in San Francisco. And then he starts on his shoes.

"Lookin' good," I tell him. "But not as good as when Capone does 'em."

My father snorts.

"Any idea what his trick is?"

"Couldn't venture a guess," my father says.

My mother is going to wear a brand-new rose-colored dress that the cons made for her in the tailor shop.

"Did a nice job, didn't they, Moose? Though I guess I should have given you a chance at it. Cam, did you know Moose likes to sew?"

"I do not, Mom, cut it out."

"That's not what I hear. According to Annie's mom, he's got a knack with a needle and thread."

"She did not say that."

"Oh yes she did. Thinks you have a hidden talent you're afraid to show."

Mothers are so embarrassing sometimes. The whole lot of them, I swear. Even so, before Natalie got accepted at the Esther P. Marinoff, my mother never would have kidded me this way. Things are changing. They really are.

After my mom is done ribbing me, she heads for Bea Trixle's, where she spends half the day getting her hair done. I know because I knocked on the door at least three times looking for Janet who still isn't back. I have to get the bar spreader off the island, for good. But I can't figure out how to do that until Janet gets home.

Only Natalie seems oblivious to all the fuss being made. Her big concern is who she can get to play button checkers with her. I don't know how Theresa knew Nat would love this game, but she did. She beats everybody every time. She's clearly a better match for herself than any of us are for her, but she likes to play with us and she gets angry if we don't give the game our all. It can't be too easy for her to win.

By nightfall, the brand-spanking clean Black Mariah sits waiting to take Hoover and Ness up to the Officers' Club and there's a hum of excitement from one end of the island to the other.

"As soon as Piper and Annie are done singing, you need to come straight back here because Mrs. Caconi will have her hands full. You understand?" my father asks as he straightens his hat.

"Yes," I say, watching my dad, wishing I could tell him what's going on.

When Nat and I get to the lately days. And I always seem to be his bad side. I hope that getting Mr. Mattaman off probation will make up for whatever else Jimmy thinks I've done wrong.

Jimmy knows what he's supposed to do. We talked it all out this afternoon. He and Theresa will help Mrs. Caconi watch Natalie while I stick by Piper.

"You won't let her throw a tantrum or anything, right?" I ask Jimmy. There's no way to prevent Natalie from throwing. We both know that.

"Theresa plays with her all the time. And if we start having problems I brought a bunch of rocks up and I'll let her sort them for my rock machine. You know she loves that," Jimmy tells me.

"Okay, then, I'm gonna go. You're all right, right?" I ask again.

Natalie jolts upright, her body suddenly rigid.

"Not you, Nat. You're going to stay here with Theresa."

Nat seems to take this in; a tiny darting smile flashes across her mouth. Theresa's whole face bursts with joy. "Did you see that, Moose? Did you? She wants to stay here with me."

When I close the Mattamans' door, Mrs. Mattaman is already gone. She went to the Officers' Club with my parents. Mr. Mattaman is on duty in the dock guard tower. Mrs. Caconi has settled in, knitting booties for the warden's new baby, Natalie is twirling a globe, and Theresa is lying on the floor, pencil in hand, ready to draw the country Nat calls. This is a new game Theresa just made up and they are having a lot of fun with it.

Everyone is content. I don't need to worry anymore.

By the time I get to the Officers' Club the place is almost completely transformed. Chairs are set up facing a main concert stage draped in blue. Piper and Annie are dressed in long velvet skirts with frilly white blouses and high heels. Piper looks elegant and grown-up. Annie looks silly, like a dressed-up domino. Her face is even more square underneath the hairdo Bea Trixle has given her.

Annie site at the piano, waiting for her cue. She is an able piano player and she can sing okay. But when Piper opens her mouth, it's scary. Pretty as she is, her singing sounds like the noise the can opener makes. My mom grinds her teeth and pinches her hand every time Piper tries for a note. It isn't just the high notes she misses either.

When Annie and Piper are finished and they've taken their bows to resounding applause by everyone except my mother. I head outside the front door to wait for them. All I can think about right now is how I can pretend I really liked their performance.

"How were we?" Piper asks when she and Annie finally make it outside, giddy and flushed from all the attention.

"Great," I tell them, trying hard to smile sincerely, "just great."

"Who dressed you tonight, Moose?" Annie asks, eyeing my suit coat and tie.

My mom got out the soap and water to wash my mouth out when she discovered all the buttons were cut off my jacket. But then she saw them in Natalie's button box and she put the soap away.

"Doesn't look like his usual self, does he?" Piper comments.

"Not a bit," Annie agrees.

Inside, we hear the tables being moved into place and the hustle of activity as the Officers' Club is transformed from a piano hall to a restaurant.

"C'mon, we need to get going," I tell Piper, and the two of us head down the stairs.

Annie lingers. "Be careful, okay?" she whispers, standing at the stairs, her back bathed in light.

The main entrance to the Officers' Club is on the second story and then you go downstairs to the "kids' door," as we call it. The kids' door is locked, but Piper has the key. She pulls it out of her pocket and unlocks the door. Annie's shadow is still on the stairs as we head inside.

No one is downstairs in the Officers' Club, but the bustle of the kitchen is right above us; dishes click, an officer gives instructions, urgent footsteps scurry across the floor.

Piper opens a cupboard in the dark back of the room. Inside is a stairwell. The officer's club used to be the post exchange (the PX) when Alcatraz was a military prison. There are little parts from what this building used to be. The kitchen is still where it was, but this back route has been boarded off at the top.

The boards were hastily nailed, leaving gaps through which we can see the pantry—and through the open pantry door to the kitchen where a man in a starched white cook's uniform whisks past carrying a plate of stuffed mushroom caps.

Was that Capone? I crane my neck to catch sight of him, but I can't see much from here. Now a man in a black jacket and white trousers brings in an empty tray. "What's next?" he asks.

"Cocktail meatballs," Willy One Arm's squeaky voice calls

as he rebalances a shiny silver tray in his one good hand.

"Get the cherries!" someone yells, and the dark closet suddenly floods with light. Piper grips my hand, her fingernails dig into my palm. Officer Bomini bends down in front of us searching the shelves.

I hold my breath, but Bomini's only concern is locating the jar of maraschino cherries, which he finds easily. When he leaves, he shuts the pantry door tightly and everything goes black.

"We need two," somebody else yells and just as suddenly the pantry door swings open again. Now we see the whole array of servers waiting to carry food. None of them look like convicts, dressed as they are in white cooks' uniforms or black dinner jackets like the wait staff of a fancy restaurant. Something is making my nose itch. Dust or maybe it's the smell of garlic. The urge to cough tickles the back of my mouth. I grind my teeth, catching the cough in the cage of my throat. I swallow it down just as Bomini's hands find the cherries and grab the jar. He's in a rush and doesn't really look. This time he leaves the door wide open.

"Number 85 you're on. This is your moment!" Officer Trixle's voice belts out. Piper squeezes my hand and for a second it seems nice to be standing so close to her as we strain to spot Capone in the bustle of waiters. He looks dapper in the black and white waiter outfit, though his starched shirt pulls across his belly. His dark black hair curls slightly around his ear as if the barber missed a strand. I can see his scar as he gathers up the plates.

"One at a time," Trixle orders. "Let's do this up good."

"The warden first?" somebody asks.

"Hoover first. Then Ness. Why not carry those two together," Officer Bomini suggests.

It's then that we see him full on—almost as if he's coming toward us. He spins so his jagged scar is in perfect line sight of our dark pantry. Quick as a flash he hawks up a good bit of phlegm and aims it straight for the potatoes on one plate, then the other. Smoothly, as if he's done this a hundred times before, he switches both plates to one hand and with his index finger swirls over the top of the mashed potatoes with a finishing twist.

"Got a problem, 85?" Associate Warden Chudley asks.

"No problem, sir. Just getting a good hold," Capone reports as he balances one plate on the flat of each palm and carries them out with the confidence of a man who has been waiting tables his whole life.

"C'mon," Piper whispers, tugging my hand.

Back we go down the stairwell as quietly as we can to the deserted first-floor bowling alley. I head for the door. Piper pulls me the other way.

"Twenty minutes, remember?" I whisper.

"It hasn't been that long."

"It has."

"We've got to see this," Piper insists.

"No." Everything inside me rises up. I won't let Piper manipulate me this way.

"We can't argue here." She yanks me past the single bowling lanes, the bag of boxing gloves, the pool cues, and up to the open front stairwell.

"Piper." I pull my arm back. "I said no."

"You don't understand how much this means to me," she

whispers. "My life is over. This is all I have." I can't tell if this is real or a performance, but either way I'm in trouble.

"Don't be ridiculous," I tell her.

"It's true. You don't know." She grabs my wrist so tightly she gives me a rope burn. "Come . . . with . . . me or I'll scream right here."

I stand my ground.

She takes a big breath. The scream starts low like a whisper—

"Wait," I tell her.

We stare at each other, just inches apart but from different sides of the universe.

"Okay, all right," I concede. What else can I do?

The main stairs are strangely quiet, like the movie theater aisle once the movie begins. At the top, she pulls us into the large formal coat closet that is full now with everyone's best coats. My stomach clenches when I see Mrs. Bomini's sweater with a needlepoint flower sewn on, Bea Trixle's beaver-collared jacket, and my mother's best white coat.

No, I won't be caught here. I spin around, but when I look back at Piper she has her mouth wide open in a silent scream and I follow her obediently again. I can't stand how Piper manipulates me, and I would never do this if I wasn't being forced, but I have to admit there's a certain thrill to being here too.

This closet is where the post office used to be when Alcatraz was an army post. Under the coats are mail slots that give us a glittering view of the whole Officers' Club clear across to the tall windows that look out on the black water and the sparkling lights of Berkeley in the distance.

The room is set up to look like a fancy restaurant with short starched white tablecloths over black floor-length cloths. Each table is set with crystal wineglasses, water glasses, dessert and bread plates, plus three forks and three spoons for each person. Warden Williams is seated right next to J. Edgar Hoover. Hoover is a mean-looking man with busy eyebrows. On the warden's other side is a young dark-haired man with a smooth face and hair parted in the middle. That's got to be Ness.

My mom and dad, Bea and Darby Trixle, and the Chudleys are also at this table. "Where's your mom?" I suddenly ask, realizing there is no seat for Mrs. Williams.

"Shhh," Piper warns.

Everyone is talking in breathy, animated party voices. Though I can't hear what they're saying, I can see from their gestures that they are all cozying up to Hoover and Ness. Bea Trixle, her hair platinum blond again today, the exact color of Mae Capone's, is watching Hoover. Even my dad is nodding to Ness as if he's just said something incredibly clever.

"Capone will serve Ness first. You'll see," Piper whispers.

Capone walks slowly but purposefully, as if he's testing out new shoes. His face is the picture of submission as he follows Officer Trixle. His hand twitches for a second in front of Ness and I wonder if he'll turn over the dinner plate and grind it into Ness's hair, but he does not. He smoothes out the tablecloth and puts down the plate with a flourish. Capone does it up; everything short of a curtsy. Then he stands at attention, his heels clicked together, watching Eliot Ness dig his fork into the spit-filled mashed potatoes.

The warden smiles his approval. His prize pig has shown well.

"Okay, we saw it. Let's get out of here," I whisper.

Piper doesn't move. "The show's not over," she says.

"You said you wanted to see Capone. You saw him. Let's go."

"No," Piper insists as Officer Trixle escorts Capone back into the kitchen and Willy One Arm appears at the head table, holding a wine bottle with a white bib tied around it. He fills each glass, finishing with a showy twist. All of which he does despite the fact that he's missing one arm and his black jacket sleeve hangs down empty flapping as he moves.

Willy catches Officer Trixle's eye. Trixle nods. Willy One Arm's good hand tosses something invisible over his shoulder as he follows Trixle into the kitchen.

"That's salt," Piper whispers. "He throws it over his shoulder after everything he does."

"Why?"

"For luck. He forgot to do it the night he lost his arm."

Trixle's lips are twitching as if there's a laugh he can't quite contain. He goes to the front podium and calls the room to attention by clinking a wineglass. "Excuse me, but we seem to have found a wallet." He opens the wallet with a flourish and takes the license out. "Says here: J. Edgar Hoover."

Hoover isn't paying attention. He's absorbed in a whispered conversation with my father.

"Lose something, Mr. Hoover?" Warden Williams asks, leaning toward J. Edgar, not a trace of humor on his face.

"Pardon me?" Hoover says.

"I said. missing something?" the warden asks.

Hoover pats at his vest, his suit coat, his trousers pockets. His dark eyebrows slide together.

Willy One Arm returns with an empty tray. Officer Trixle sweeps a folded napkin through the air and places it carefully on the tray. Then he sets the wallet right in the center and Willy One Arm scurries over to J. Edgar Hoover, whose mouth is even more dour than it was before. Hoover snatches his wallet back, checks the contents, and slips it into his vest pocket in one swift motion like a rodent who has found his cheese.

"Guess you got your pocket picked on Alcatraz, sir," Warden Williams says as he spreads a thick coat of butter on his bread, careful not to look Mr. Hoover in the face. "Like I said this afternoon, Mr. Hoover, we have the the cleverest criminals in the whole country here on Alcatraz. I think it would be a bad idea to cut back our guard forces . . . a bad idea indeed."

27. THROW, CATCH, THROW, CATCH

▪ ▪

Same day—Sunday, September 8, 1935

I finally get Piper out of there, back down the stairs and into the bowling alley basement again. "Can you believe that?" she whispers.

"Ness ate Capone's spit. You know how he shines Trixle's shoes? Bet that's the trick."

"A spit shine?" She asks with a whispery laugh.

"Willy was amazing. I didn't even see his hand move. Did you?" I whisper as we let ourselves out into the dark night, lit by a full moon and the bright entrance light. As the cold air hits me, I suddenly stare stupidly at Piper. How are we going to get back to 64 without the guard in the dock tower spotting us? Why didn't I think this through?

"How are we going to get back?" I ask. Piper can make these kinds of mistakes. I can't.

"We could shimmy down the wall and walk in the water," Piper suggests.

"Mattaman will shoot us. He'll think we're escaping cons."

"Maybe. Maybe not," Piper says.

I roll my eyes. How can she be so blasé about this. It's almost as if she wants to be caught. "We could throw a rock over in the wrong direction. Mattaman will point his guns on that spot and we'll run," I offer.

"Throwing stuff . . . that's your solution to everything, isn't it?" Piper whispers.

"Got a better idea?"

She shakes her head. "Nope."

A sheet of sweat forms on my forehead. We stare at the guard tower. We can probably get back behind my dad's electrical shop without Mattaman seeing us, but once we get close to 64, there's almost no way to get back without being spotted. Still, I can't just stand here and wait until my father comes out. I have to get back to Natalie.

The first rock makes no sound. The second rock is big and soft—more of a dirt clod, it hits with a thud and splits apart, unloading a pile of dirt on the newly washed road.

We don't have time to worry about this, we just run. My legs rip across the road and up behind my dad's electrical shop. Now we're safely out of sight of the tower, but then I see where we have to go.

To get to 64 now, we have to run within clear sight of Mattaman; there's no way we won't get caught. I'm breathing hard from the run. So is Piper. I'll bet she's thinking what I'm thinking. We're dead meat now.

"We got to pretend we're supposed to be here," she says.

"No," I say.

"Let me handle it," she says, darting across the clear bull's-eye window between the electrical shop and 64. .

Within seconds, Mattaman's high-powered searchlight finds her, and I scuttle out to where she's standing.

"Piper? Moose?" he calls through the bullhorn. "What's going on down there?"

"Just coming back from playing for Mr. Hoover, Mr. Mattaman," Piper calls back.

"Thought you were done earlier," Mattaman bellows.

"No, sir," Piper answers.

"That right, Moose?" Mattaman calls down.

My heart beats loudly in my ears, flushing me with guilt. "Yes, sir," I say weakly.

Piper walks in her usual sure-of-herself manner. I follow suit down the stairs of the 64 building.

When we arrive at the Mattamans', Piper cracks a big smile. "I'm so good," she says.

Doesn't she ever feel ashamed, I wonder as Mrs. Caconi pounces on us, her face red and shiny with sweat. "Do you have her?" she cries.

"Who? Have who?" I ask, but I already know the answer. I can feel it in the tightening of my belly and the dizziness in my head.

"I don't know what happened, Moose." Mrs. Caconi's lip begins trembling. "One minute Natalie was here. The next minute she was gone. Jimmy and Theresa are out looking for her. But you'd know where she'd have got to. Course you do!" She mops her forehead with her handkerchief.

"I better go get my parents," I say.

"Oh now, Moose. . . you don't need to go and do that, do ya? Go on. You'll find her. I know you will," Mrs. Caconi's big pink hand is on my back, pushing me out the door.

"She doesn't want us to tell," Piper blurts out as we run down the balcony. "She doesn't want to get in trouble either."

I try to figure out where Natalie would go.

"Let's try the swings," I say as we head up the stairs to the parade grounds, though I wonder if I should get my parents. I don't want to tell them I wasn't with Natalie, but this is serious.

We round the corner of 64 building and slam into Jimmy and Theresa. They're panting like they've just run a few miles.

"Natalie?" my voice croaks.

Jimmy is doubled over with a side ache. "We checked behind 64 building, Chinatown, the parade grounds. Nothing."

"I was in the bathroom," Theresa explains in a high voiceh. "*Jimmy* was supposed to be watching her."

Jimmy puts his head in his hands. "Two minutes I was gone. I just went to get the ball. It went over the railing," he mutters miserably.

"That's all you ever do. Throw and catch. Throw and catch," Theresa practically shouts at him.

"Shut up, Theresa. Let's just find Natalie," Piper tells her.

"Where would Natalie go?" I try to think, but my mind is jammed with fear.

"The secret passageway?" Piper whispers.

"She doesn't know about it." Then it comes to me, what I told her yesterday: *tomorrow. We can see Molly tomorrow.* "Your house," I tell Piper.

Theresa's head is like a little nodding machine. "She kept talking about that mouse, Molly."

"Why didn't you tell me that before?" Jimmy shouts at her.

Theresa takes a big wobbly breath. "Don't yell at me. I didn't think of it."

I'm already running up the steps with Piper right behind me. Mattaman can see us here too, only not as easily or as clearly. But right now I don't care about Mattaman. I just want to find Natalie.

We tear up out of the tower guard's sight lines and take the shortcut to Piper's house. At least the pass men won't be at the warden's house. Thank God they don't work at night.

When we get to Piper's doorstep, heaving from the uphill run, Piper pulls open the door, slips inside, and slams the door in my face. "Wait here," her muffled voice barks from inside the house.

"Hey." I shove open the door.

"No!" She squeezes it shut again and turns the lock.

I pound on the door. "Piper!" I yell. Then I run around to the back door and shove myself against it. This door opens easily and I almost fall into the kitchen.

A bed has been moved inside the large kitchen along with bags of fluids and containers of pills. Mrs. Williams is lying on the bed, a thin cover over her enormous stomach, her skin as gray as dead fish, and a smell like overripe peaches is hanging in the air. Doc Ollie's sister is running a washcloth across Piper's mom's forehead.

"Moose?" Doc Ollie's sister looks up in surprise.

"I found her! She's here!" Piper yells from another part of the house. Relief shoots through my system.

I duck out the back door, but not fast enough. Piper has run around the house looking for me. She sees me come out the back door.

"I told you not to go in." Piper's voice drops suddenly as Natalie comes around the house.

"Natalie," I say, so glad to see her, my insides ache with relief.

"I told you!" Piper shouts.

"Yeah but—" I mumble, staring at Piper, whose face is half lit by the glow of the big yellow moon.

"Stop looking like that!" She shoves me.

"Like what?" I mutter, wondering how I'm supposed to look.

"Stop!" Piper's nails are ready to scratch my eyes out. "My mom is fine. Buddy said so." Her voice breaks.

"Okay," I whisper.

It's quiet up here—a world away from the party below. Only the sound of the night crickets and a distant boat horn. Piper looks as if she might burst. "Hey, I believe you," I whisper in my most soothing voice.

Piper lunges at me again. "She is."

"Okay, all right." I lift my arms in the cool night air.

Tears stream down Piper's face. "I told you to stop looking that way! She's fine!" Piper sobs. "She's just going to have a baby. That's all." Piper is crumpled over like an empty dress. "Say it!" she cries, her voice choked with sobs.

"She's fine, Piper," I tell her. Natalie is rocking from one foot to another, her eyes scanning Piper and then the ground, Piper and then the ground.

Piper's eyes spit like bacon on the griddle. "You think you know everything. But you don't. Everyone hates you, Moose."

"Everyone hates you, Moose," Nat repeats. "Not Natalie. Not me," Nat mutters, touching her chest.

Piper ignores Natalie. "Jimmy does. You treat him like an imbecile because he doesn't like baseball."

"I don't treat him like a—"

"Why do you think he's trying so hard to learn to play?"

I grind my teeth.

"Yeah. Annie's teaching him. And Annie . . . you only like her because she has a great throwing arm."

"There are lots of things I like about Annie," I whisper. "Piper, you're just upset. Don't take it out on me."

"Yeah, name one. Name one thing you like about Annie."

"She's nice. She's smart. I can trust her."

"If she couldn't play baseball, you wouldn't be her friend."

"That's not true."

"Yeah, it is, and Scout hates you because you're always sure he's after me."

"Well, he is after you."

"You don't know anything, do you?" she lashes out at me. "You're a complete moron like your sister. It runs in your family." She glares at Natalie, the tears streaming down her face.

"You're a moron!" Piper screams at Natalie.

"Shut up!" I can't help myself. Nobody says this to Natalie. Nobody. But then the scene in the kitchen flashes through my mind. The gray, sick, drawn face. The sickly sweet rotting smell.

"What's wrong with your mom, Piper?" I whisper.

"Nothing!" she screams. "*Nothing is wrong!*"

But the louder she screams, the more she sees I don't believe her. She shoves me away. "Can't you see, you moron? Nothing is wrong!" She turns and runs back into the house.

When Natalie and I get back down to 64 building, Mrs. Mattaman is waiting for us outside our apartment. I'm not sure what Mrs. Mattaman knows and what she doesn't know, but from the way her eyes are squinting and her foot is tapping, she's clearly hopping mad. "Go straight to bed, you two." Her voice is cold and hard. "I will be back in half an hour to check on you, and you had better be in bed snoring, do you understand me?

"When Mr. Mattaman gets off at eight tomorrow morning you, Moose, will report to our apartment. You and Theresa and Jimmy have major explaining to do, you hear me? Pulling shenanigans on an important night like this . . . shame on you!" She waves her fancy jeweled purse at me.

"Mrs. Mattaman?" I ask as she turns to leave. "Is Piper's mom okay?"

Mrs. Mattaman stops, her chest heaving. "I dunno, Moose," she says without turning back. "I really don't know."

28. PIG HALF IN THE POKE

■ ■

Monday, September 9, 1935

The next morning when I wake up, Natalie is staring over me, peering into my eyes like she's doing a wake-up spell.

"What is it?" I ask.

Natalie says nothing, but I can see by the way she's digging her chin in her chest that she's anxious.

I wonder what she made of what happened last night. Did she know she wasn't supposed to go to the warden's house? Did she understand why Piper was yelling at me? Does she know what the word *moron* means? It would be a lot easier to feel sad for Piper if she wasn't so mean.

Natalie stays with me as if she is suddenly glued to my side. I have to go in the bathroom and close the door in her face to get changed. When I'm done, she's waiting right outside.

In the kitchen, we hear my dad rattling around. What does he know about last night, I wonder. I'd rather he find out about it from me, but maybe he won't have to hear about it at all. Maybe the Mattamans will want to keep this quiet. Mrs. Caconi too. I'm sure she'd prefer if my parents didn't know Natalie disappeared on her watch.

"What's your plan this morning?" Natalie asks when she sees our dad.

We both look at her as if the stove just spoke. Slowly, my father's face changes from surprise to pleasure.

"Gonna make myself some breakfast," he tells Natalie. "And you, sweet pea?"

"Moose," she mutters. "Stay with Moose."

"Mrs. Mattaman invited us over," I tell him.

"For breakfast?" He cocks his head and sets the coffeepot down.

"Uh-huh. Dad, what's happening with Mrs. Williams?"

My dad shrugs. "It's hard to know. The warden likes to play things close to the vest."

My mother pokes her head in the kitchen.

"Piper's mom . . . is she okay?" I ask her.

My mother rubs her eyes and tightens the cord on her bathrobe. "We're all worried." She sighs. "You hear something?"

I can't tell her what I saw without explaining what in the heck I was doing up there. I wish I could, though. I really wish I could.

At the Mattamans' the first person we see is Riv Mattaman. The whites of his eyes are shot through with pink and his legs are kicked over the arm of the chair, as if he's too tired to sit the normal way. Mattaman did a shift and a half in the guard tower. No wonder he's beat.

He groans when he sees me, which makes me feel like crap. I can't meet his bloodshot eyes.

Nat sits right down to a game of button checkers already in process from last night. She looks up at Theresa, her eyes full of longing, but Theresa has hold of her dad's hand and won't let it go. Natalie reluctantly settles in to play by herself.

"Piper's not here, Dad." Theresa pulls on his arm. "You can't start till *she* gets here."

"Mind your own business, missy," he tells Theresa, then looks at all of us. "What the heck happened last night?"

Jimmy takes a step forward. "Piper got you and Moose's dad in trouble because she was mad at Theresa."

"I didn't do anything! It wasn't me," Theresa cries.

"Was so.," Jimmy glares at her.

Mattaman pulls at his still crisply creased pant leg and rests his foot on the chair rung. "Come again?" he asks.

"She told the warden she saw you and Mr. Flanagan drinking just before you went on duty."

In the kitchen, Mrs. Mattaman slams her rolling pin down, then yanks her apron off, wads it up, tosses it on the chair, and marches into the living room.

"She said she'd get you out of trouble if Moose would help her meet Capone," Jimmy explains. "So she and Moose snuck back inside to watch."

"That true?" Mr. Mattaman directs his question at me.

"Yes, sir. We saw Capone spit in Eliot Ness's mashed potatoes. He hocked up a gob of phlegm, then he smoothed it over with his finger. Gave it a little swirl. I saw with my own eyes."

Mr. Mattaman pulls at his mustache.

Theresa makes a face. "Ouuuu," she says.

"But Natalie didn't go with you. It was just you and Piper in there?" Mr. Mattaman asks.

"While they were gone, we were watching Natalie with Mrs. Caconi," Jimmy explains, "but Nat snuck out. She went to the warden's house."

"She wanted to see Molly, the mouse Willy One Arm has," Theresa adds.

Mr. Mattaman points at her. "And you, missy? What did you do that annoyed Piper so much that started this whole thing?"

Theresa's lower lip puckers up. "Nothing. Piper is the wrong one, not me."

Jimmy snorts. "C'mon, Theresa." He glares at his sister, then turns to his dad. "She spies on us, Dad. And she can't stand that Moose likes Piper."

The blood rushes to my face. "I do not like Piper."

"Do so," Theresa says.

"Theresa! Since when is that your business? You and I need to have a talk about this in private," Mr. Mattaman tells her. Theresa's mouth droops.

"And you two." he points at me and Jimmy. "Why didn't you tell me about this? For Pete's sake—" He sighs, his brown eyes softening. "Since when do you think you run the place?"

"Can I ask one little tiny teeny question?" Theresa's hand is up by her face like she's not sure whether to raise it all the way or not. "When are you going to talk to Piper?"

"Listen up, Theresa. I'm not going to say this twice. This . . . is . . . not . . . your . . . business."

Her shoulders slump down. "If it was my business, would you tell me?"

"Theresa Maria Mattaman." Riv's voice gathers steam.

"Okay, okay." She puts her hand down.

"All right then. I don't want news of these shenanigans to go farther than this room, do you understand me?" He points to each of us and we nod.

"And if I ever hear of any of you taking matters into your own hands, again, I will go straight to the warden. Is that understood?" Mr. Mattaman looks around the room again, checking in with each of us.

We all nod our heads. Even Theresa. Only Natalie continues to play checkers, one lone player against herself. In the silence of our head nodding, she looks up at us and down again.

On the way back from the Mattamans', Nat walks even slower than normal, dragging her foot on the ground, running her hand along the wall and humming an empty tune.

"What's the matter, Nat?" I ask her.

"Peoples are mad at Moose," she says.

I hold the door of our place open waiting for her to come in. "Yeah, but it's okay. We got off easy—practically scot-free."

She touches her own chest. "No one is mad at Natalie. Natalie is a moron."

"No, Nat, listen to me. Listen very closely." My chest wells up. "You're not a moron. Piper is . . . She's the moron. Not you."

"Mr. Mattaman shakes his finger at Moose. Not Natalie. Natalie went away."

"Yeah, you shouldn't do that, Nat. You shouldn't go up to the warden's house," I tell her. "But could we discuss this inside?"

"Why?" she asks, suddenly looking directly at me.

"Because it's not safe to go to the warden's house and I don't want to talk about this out here on the balcony where people can hear."

"Tomorrow, we can see Molly tomorrow. Moose said," she whispers.

"Yeah, okay, I said that. But I was wrong. We can't go up

there whenever we want. There are things you can't do. You can't go up top and"—my voice drops down—"you can't be friends with 105 either."

"105," she mutters.

"Does he visit you, Natalie?"

"Visitors, Natalie. Mommy is here," she says the way Sadie would say it, only quieter.

"Yeah, Mom visits, but does 105 visit?" I whisper.

"Dad visits," Nat says.

"Mom and Dad visit, but 105 *doesn't* visit."

"105 *doesn't* visit," she mimics.

She's not just repeating what I said, right? "But how did you get the stuff in your suitcase?"

"Sadie packs my suitcase," she says.

"Sadie packed the bar spreader?" I whisper, my throat suddenly too small for my words.

Natalie doesn't answer. She's busy counting the posts in the porch rail.

"C'mon, Nat!" Again, nothing.

"Nat, Please. Let's get inside," I plead. "Mom! Dad!" I call in the door, but it's silent—too silent—inside. Where did they go?

"Natalie." I'm begging now. Something about the way she seems to have locked up in place is making me very nervous.

"Home Moose. Not home Natalie," she says.

It's Monday, but she's not going back to the Esther P. Marinoff for another week. Some kind of teacher break before the fall semester.

"Moose go. Natalie stay," she mutters, closing her eyes and spinning round and round like a merry-go-round pushing herself faster and faster, until she falls in a clump on the balcony.

"Natalie, not here, okay? Just get inside." But she doesn't move. She is curled up in a ball frozen there.

"Moose!" a bullhorn bleats. But it isn't Darby. It's Janet.

"Leave us alone, Janet," I call down to her, but as soon as I say this, Darby appears by the first-floor landing.

"What's going on?" he bellows into his bullhorn. It blasts loud enough for all of 64 to hear.

"Nothing, sir," I say.

"Don't look like nothin' to me, son."

Mrs. Chudley opens her window. Mrs. Caconi comes out, her hands on her big hips. She still looks exhausted from last night. Bea's clickety-clackety high heels sound on the stairs.

"Sure ain't normal what she's doin' now," Darby bellows.

"C'mon, Nat. Let's get you inside." I try to scoop her up, but I can't get her to move.

"Where are your folks?" Darby's voice echoes in the bullhorn.

"Natalie," I whisper, "we need to count the dishes. Come inside." This is lame, but it's all I can think of.

Nat doesn't budge. Her eyes are shut tight.

"Natalie, we need you to come and check . . . Mom's knitting something for the warden's baby. You need to help," I lie. My mother doesn't know how to knit.

Still nothing.

Out of the corner of my eye I see Janet Trixle banging on the Mattamans' door. "C'mon, Theresa! Jimmy! Moose needs help!" she bellows in her baby bullhorn.

"Janet! You come down here!" Darby shouts, but it's too late. Janet has Theresa and Jimmy in tow. Jimmy takes one look at

Natalie and understands exactly what's going on.

"Let's carry her in," Jimmy says. He scoops up her arms, Theresa gets her feet, and I carry her middle. It's awkward, but it's not far, only a few feet really. We manage to lug her over the threshold of our apartment and close the door.

I can't believe it's Janet helping, but it is. "Thanks," I tell all of them.

Janet's face glows. "You want to play?" she whispers to Theresa.

Theresa looks at me. I nod.

"'Kay," Theresa says as she, Jimmy, and Janet go out. I breathe a huge sigh of relief as I close the door after them.

"Jeez, Natalie. I wish you wouldn't do that," I tell my sister, who is curled up in a ball like a potato bug.

At least she's quiet. It could be a lot worse, I'm thinking, when I hear a knock on the door.

"Moose, can I come in?" Darby Trixle wipes his feet on the mat and steps inside without waiting for my answer.

"Uh, Officer Trixle, sir, my parents aren't here right now," I say, but it's too late, he's headed straight for our sofa.

"It's you I want to have the conversation with. How's she doin'?" He eyes Natalie, who is still curled up on the floor.

"Fine, sir," I whisper.

"She ain't fine, Moose. Now you look here. She ain't no reflection on you. I want you to know that."

"Yes, sir," I say, wishing he would just leave, but he settles in on the couch.

He pokes his chin in Natalie's direction. "Happens in families sometimes. You think I don't know how it is, but I do, see. I had me a brother wasn't right in the head. But my folks they did the right thing. Put him away with his own kind. And we got a clean slate. He was happier for it, we all were. That's the way to do it. Get a clean slate."

He waits for me to respond. "Yes, sir," I finally mutter.

"A girl like her. She don't belong. And this visiting back and forth." He waggles his head. "Can't have a pig half in the poke . . . you know what I'm saying?"

I look down at the coffee table, wishing I could pull it out from under his feet.

"You look at me when I'm speaking to you, boy."

"Yes, sir," I mutter

He squints his eyes at me. "You ought to be taught right about this."

I can feel the anger grow inside me, until it just about bursts out of my skin. "Officer Trixle, sir?" I struggle to keep my voice under control. "Do you visit your brother?"

"That's what I'm saying boy." He says this louder now, like I'm too stupid to understand. "You make a *clean* break. He got his life. I got mine."

"So you never visit. Ever," I whisper.

"You just move on from the bad things. You understand me, boy."

"She's not a bad thing," I whisper.

"You and your parents is too soft." He clucks. "I blame your dad. Women can't see these things right. They don't got the power up here." He points to his head. "But your dad, he's got his head where his arse ought to be. I'm not gonna have you putting this whole island in jeopardy, because you people is soft in the head, you hear me?"

"Yes, sir," I whisper. "I hear you, but she's not soft in the head."

"You Flanagans"—he spits into his hanky, wads it up and stuffs it in his pocket—"can't see the forest for the trees. It's a shame really," he mutters softly, almost gently. "I feel bad for you. I do."

29. A SWEET SPOT FOR MOOSE

∎∎∎∎∎∎∎∎∎∎∎∎∎∎∎∎∎∎∎∎∎∎∎∎∎∎∎∎∎∎∎∎∎∎∎∎

Monday, September 9, and Tuesday, September 10, 1935

When my mom gets back, she stays with Natalie. The two of them hole up in Nat's room, Nat lying on the bed, her arms tucked under her as if she's flown apart and she's bringing herself together again. Fits exhaust Natalie. They exhaust my mom too. Sometimes it seems like there's still an umbilical cord between them.

After I get home from school the next day I head for the canteen with Annie, Jimmy, and Theresa. Jimmy doesn't say much. He helped me with Natalie when she was having her fit, but he still feels bad about not keeping his eyes on her the night Hoover was here. He goes down to check his flies, which now occupy two barrels under the dock. But he doesn't invite me down there anymore.

While Jimmy's gone, Theresa and Annie and I help Bea unpack boxes. There really isn't that much to do.

Late in the afternoon, Mrs. Mattaman, Mrs. Caconi, Annie's mom, Bea and Janet Trixle come sweeping into the canteen, practically clearing out the baking aisle. Even Mrs. Caconi, who never buys from the canteen because she thinks the prices are too high, gets butter and eggs.

"What's going on, Mom?" Jimmy asks.

"Bea's closing up early so we can get the baking done."

"Why's everybody baking?" Theresa asks.

"Never you mind. You kids just run along." She waggles her fingers toward the door. "Outside with all of you."

Janet turns the wooden sign to CLOSED. She gives Theresa a smug little smile. "We're going up to Mrs. Caconi's apartment because little pitchers have big ears," Janet whispers to Theresa.

"What's that supposed to mean?" Theresa asks me.

"It means they don't want us to hear what they're going to say. But that's what secret passageways are for, Theresa," I tell her.

Theresa smiles big as a Halloween pumpkin. There's a skip to her step as she, Annie, Jimmy, and I head for Chinatown. Jimmy unscrews the screws that hold the hinge and we scramble inside. "Shhh!" he orders. "We know they're up there."

"Icky!" Theresa whispers, whacking a cobweb out of her face.

"Quiet or you can't come," Jimmy warns.

By the time we get settled at the best eavesdropping spot, the women are already in Mrs. Caconi's living room.

"Now you mustn't talk that way. She's gonna pull through," Annie's mom says.

"Janet, you stay in the bedroom like I told you. Play with your dollies, all right?" Bea tells Janet. "I know a death rattle when I hear it. That woman is not long for this world." Bea sighs. "I wish I could say I didn't see this coming. I mean, the doctor told her not to have anymore."

"Oh now, Bea, these things happen," Mrs. Mattaman tells her.

"Well, you're not going to tell me he didn't want a boy more than life itself." Bea again.

"No guarantees it's gonna be a boy," Mrs. Caconi offers.

"Try telling the warden that," Bea says. "Got him signed up for military school and the sailing club already."

"That's up to God, not the warden," Annie's mom insists.

"I'll tell you what's up to us," Mrs. Mattaman declares. "Piper. I'll be the first to tell you she's not my favorite child. But right now she's all alone in that big house with her mama rushed off to the hospital sick enough to . . ." She takes a deep breath. "It's not right. Somebody has to go up there with her."

"I'll go," Mrs. Caconi offers. "I can cook in the warden's kitchen same as mine."

"Now let's hold our horses here, girls, and use our noggins. Who's the closest friend Piper's got?" Bea asks.

"Moose," Mrs. Mattaman replies.

"Ain't that the truth," Bea answers. "Those two and their googly eyes. Where is he?"

"We sent them out to play. Get them out of our hair," Annie's mom says.

"That boy, my goodness. If there's a hand that needs a-holdin' he's the one for the job. I'll be darned if he didn't get me a rose one day when I was feeling down. Still can't figure that one out," Bea says.

"He's a nice boy. That's what. My Annie thinks the world of him," Mrs. Bomini says.

"Got a sweet spot for Moose is what your Annie has," Bea answers.

Annie's mom sighs. "I'm afraid so. But enough of that now, girls. We've got our work cut out for us."

"Annie," Theresa whispers, "you have a crush on Moose?"

But Annie is gone. She's weaseled past Jimmy. She's crawling like a spider down the passage to the door, which opens with a squeal and closes with a crump. We can hear her distant footsteps running up the cement stairway that leads out of Chinatown.

My cheeks get hot with the thought that Annie has a crush on me. I don't like her in that way. I mean, Annie? She's a box with feet. But it's kind of nice to think she likes me—so long as it doesn't affect her pitching, that is.

But then I hear my name again and I can't think about Annie because I want to listen to what the ladies at Mrs. Caconi's are saying about me.

"Well, I'm gonna go find Moose and send him up there. We can't leave that child scared out of her wits and all alone. Poor little thing," Mrs. Mattaman says.

"You find Moose, we'll get the baking going. Then we'll figure out who goes to visit poor June," Bea commands.

"Get outta here, Moose, fast as you can," Jimmy whispers. He moves out of the way and I crawl back to the door and jump out with Theresa on my tail. I take the Chinatown stairs two at a time and run into Mrs. Mattaman as she heads out to the parade grounds.

"There you are, Moose," Mrs. Mattaman says as Theresa catches up. "And Theresa, you may as well hear this too."

Theresa grabs her mom's hand and holds it tight.

"Mrs. Williams is sick. They took her to St. Luke's Hospital in the city. She may not . . . She's very sick."

"She may not what?" Theresa asks.

"Now, never you mind," Mrs. Mattaman tells her.

"What about the baby?" I ask.

Mrs. Mattaman heaves a big breath. "Don't know yet about the baby." Her voice breaks.

"I knew it," Theresa whispers.

"You knew what?" Mrs. Mattaman strokes Theresa's tumble of black curls.

"She's not even going to get in trouble now,." Theresa insists.

"Who isn't?"

"Piper."

"Theresa!" Mrs. Mattaman snaps. "That poor girl may lose her mommy. You're old enough to know what that means. Whether or not she should have been balled out is beside the point."

"No, it's not," Theresa whispers.

"Shame on you." Mrs. Mattaman's jaw sets, her dark eyes fire up. "You wipe that look off your face, young lady, and march back home and wash your mouth out with soap."

Theresa's steps are heavy as she heads for home.

Mrs. Mattaman sighs. "She has a big heart for every other creature on God's green earth, but she sure can't find it in herself to be kind to Piper.

"Now, Moose." She focuses her attention back on me. "I know your mom's got her hands full with Natalie, so I'm going to step up to the plate. You get yourself up to the warden's house, young man. Piper needs a friend. Oh boy, does she ever. And if you can't forgive her, well, shame on you, too. There isn't a friend in the world won't disappoint you one day. You going to hold a grudge, you'll have a mighty lonely life."

"I could get Annie. Wouldn't this be a better girl job?" I

suggest.

Mrs. Mattaman looks at me intently. "C'mon now, Moose. I think we both know Piper would rather see you."

My eyes don't meet Mrs. Mattaman's. I hate to admit she's right. "What do you say to someone whose mother is that sick?" I ask.

Mrs. Mattaman seals her lips up tight and nods her head. "It's not what you say, Moose. Not one word any of us says is going to help that poor child right now. But you go up there and you stay with her. That's what she'll remember. That we loved her enough to go through this with her. We're a family here on Alcatraz and that's what families do. Now you go on."

"Yes, ma'am," I say.

"And, Moose? You want to bring her back down to our place, you go right ahead. She's welcome. You bet she is."

30. WHY ARE BOYS SPECIAL?

= =

Same day—Tuesday, September 10, 1935

I have walked as slowly as possible up the switchback, but even at this pace I get there before I want to. I drag myself up the steps to Piper's front door and push the bell. Willy One Arm answers with Molly on his shoulder. He makes the sign of the cross, his empty sleeve flapping in the breeze.

I follow Willy into the dark living room. The drapes are shut tight. No light shines anywhere. And the smell of sickness is all around like bandages and rotting fruit. I wonder why Willy can't get rid of the smell. Men are no good at cleaning even with two arms, my mom says.

I don't even begin to know what I'm going to say to Piper. And I'm a little annoyed with Mrs. Mattaman for sending me on this impossible mission. Why is it I'm the one everyone always decides can handle these things?

It's the curse of niceness, I swear.

"What are you doing? Go away." Piper's voice comes from the shadowy stairwell where she sits, huddled on a step.

My hand forms a fist around a nickel shoved deep in my pocket. "Why don't you come down to the canteen? I'll buy you a pop," I suggest.

"I heard it's closed."

"It is."

"Then why'd you ask?"

"Bea Trixle will open the canteen."

"Not if it's closed."

"For you she will—"

"Oh," Piper says in a voice so small it sounds like somebody stepped on it.

I don't know what to do with myself or what to say. Maybe I'll just open my mouth and hope the right words come out.

"Piper, what's your, um . . . What are they going to name the baby?"

Piper's eyes are closed and she's leaning back on the steps. I think she isn't going to answer and then her eyelids flutter.

"It," she whispers.

"Your parents are going to name the baby It?"

"I'm going to call him It."

"It Williams. Were you thinking of a middle name?" I ask.

"Ee-It," she says.

"It Ee-It Williams?"

"Yep, Idiot Williams." Piper smiles, which feels to me like a small victory.

But now what do I say? "Mrs. Mattaman had Rocky and it all worked out okay, Piper." This is the only thing I can think of to say.

"Mrs. Mattaman didn't get sick like this."

"No," I concede, "she didn't."

"I wanted *It Ee-it* to die. Not my mom." Her voice catches.

I put my arm around Piper. It feels like there's no place for my arm on her shoulder. Why is it when you see this done in the movies, it looks so natural?

"The best, the very best I could hope for is . . ." Her voice breaks. ". . . a little sister like Theresa Mattaman. That is pretty bad."

"C'mon, Piper. Theresa's okay."

"Theresa's a brat."

"You could do a whole lot worse than Theresa Mattaman."

"Yeah." She glares at me. "I could end up with a Natalie."

"A Natalie?" I take my arm back. My teeth grind so hard I'm pulverizing them to dust in my mouth.

"What gives you the right to say something like that? I'm trying to be nice here and you just turn on me."

Piper snorts. "You can't even say you're looking forward to her going back."

"Because I'm not."

"Yeah, you are. And so is your mom."

"Shut up!" I shout.

"You're not as nice as you pretend to be, you know."

"I'm not pretending." My voice squeezes out of my chest.

Piper is staring off in another direction, oblivious to how much she's hurt me. "My dad wants a son." Her voice is thick. "Why are boys so special anyway?"

"We can do more things."

"Annie plays ball as well as you do."

"No, she doesn't."

"Yes, she does. It's not fair," Piper says.

I snort. "Lots of things aren't fair. Are you just now finding this out?" I ask, still stinging from her comment about Natalie.

"They should be. Everything should be fair," she says, the

tears spilling over. Her hands try to push them back, wipe them off, make them go away.

"Come on," I tell her. I want to get away from this dark and silent house, away from the smell of sickness and away from Piper, but I know Mrs. Mattaman will have my head if I leave her here. "Let's go down to the Mattamans'," I suggest.

"They don't like me."

"They shouldn't like you," I say. "After what you did, they should hate your guts. But they don't."

"I don't want to go."

"Too bad," I tell her.

She squints at me. I don't think she's going to move, but she does. She gets up and follows me out the door.

Mr. and Mrs. Mattaman are both in their kitchen doing dishes when Piper and I arrive. I swing through the door first. Piper, a few lengths behind me, walks slower and slower like she hopes never to reach their apartment.

For a second the shadow of something dark crosses Mrs. Mattaman's face, but then it's gone and she dries her hand on her apron and hurries out to where Piper is now reluctantly wiping her feet on the Mattamans' doormat.

She gathers Piper into her arms. Piper seems to crumble, like a log burned to the core. She folds into Mrs. Mattaman as if she's been holding herself together until this very moment.

Mrs. Mattaman's lips press together until they are almost purple. She cradles Piper between her two short arms and ushers her into the warm living room with its good baking smells.

On the couch Piper gasps for air. Mrs. Mattaman holds her while she cries.

It's probably only a minute or two, but the sound is like nothing I've ever heard before.

"Now, now." Mrs. Mattaman strokes Piper's head gently and lovingly. Piper Williams, the girl who tried to get her husband fired.

Mr. Mattaman is in the living room now too. Piper's face seems to crumble all over again when she sees him. She buries her head in Mrs. Mattaman's lap. But then something inside of her forces her head up.

She grabs hold of her arms, wraps them around herself. Her eyes dart toward Mr. Mattaman. "You were never drunk," she whispers, the sadness making her tongue too thick for her mouth. "I guess you know that."

"Yes," Mrs. Mattaman says softly. She has hold of Mr. Mattaman's hand now too, like the three of them are linked in something larger than themselves.

The tears flow across Piper's face like water lapping against the dock. "I'm . . ." Piper is trying to say something else, but she can't get the words out because her chest is heaving too hard. "Sorry," she finally says as Theresa comes in, her hands on her hips, her mouth ready to burst.

"Theresa." Mrs. Mattaman lets go of Piper and holds a hand out to Theresa. "Piper has apologized. We've forgiven her, haven't we?"

Theresa looks from her mother to her father, both of whom are directing their chins up and down as if they are nodding for her. Theresa's mouth opens to object, but the force of her parents' will carries her head along. She nods in the same beat and time as they do.

Piper is curled up next to Mrs. Mattaman on the couch with Theresa on Mrs. Mattaman's other side. Piper puts her head on Mrs. Mattaman's lap and falls fast asleep with Mrs. Mattaman's hand on her hair.

31. THE WARDEN'S PARTY

■■■■■■■■■■■■■■■■■■■■■■■■■■■■■■■■

Friday, September 13, 1935

It's tense this week on the island. No one knows what's happening with Piper's mom, and the warden spends all of his time at the hospital. With Warden Williams gone, Associate Warden Chudley is in charge. But the warden has never left his post before, so Chudley has no idea how to handle the island without him. In the kitchen, I hear my dad and mom discussing this. "Can't make a decision which shoe to put on first," my dad tells my mom. "He shouldn't be in charge. Let's just hope nothing happens . . ."

Luckily on Friday, when Jimmy and I get back from school, the warden is down at the dock. "A boy! It's a boy!" he crows, handing out cigars to every man, no matter his rank. "I have a son! Walter, his name is Walter William Williams." His voice full of joy, his big face beaming with delight, he looks like another person entirely.

"What happened with Piper's mom?" Jimmy whispers.

"Beats me," I say.

It's not until Jimmy and I get to the Mattamans' apartment that we find out the full story.

"It was touch and go, but it looks like Mrs. Williams is gonna make it," Mrs. Mattaman tells us from the kitchen where she is cleaning celery. "That got lost in the warden's report, did it?" Mrs. Mattaman lays the celery out and works her knife across it with a rising vengeance.

"Was Piper at school, Moose?" Mrs. Mattaman asks without looking up from her work.

I nod. "This morning she was, but she didn't come home with us."

"Course it's none of my business." Mrs. Mattaman chops faster. "But why the warden felt the need to bring his son home, while his wife is still in the hospital"—*chop, chop, chop*—"I will never understand. You'd think he gave birth to that baby by himself."

"Where's the baby now?" Jimmy asks.

"Mrs. Caconi is watching him. But all this morning the warden was parading him up one side of the island and down the other." Mrs. Mattaman shakes her head. "And now he's throwing a party. Why he couldn't wait until June got home I will never understand." Mrs. Mattaman points her knife at us. "You didn't hear that . . . either one of you."

"Yes, ma'am," we tell her as she dumps the celery into a giant burbling pot that smells like garlic and tomato sauce.

Outside we see Bea Trixle hauling out cartons of beer for the grown-ups and root beer for the kids. Mrs. Chudley has her accordion and begins to play.

Soon, Mr. and Mrs. Bomini are dancing on the balcony of 64 building and even my mom goes up to the Officers' Club and plays requests for the warden, who is giddy with happiness. His son in his arms, he waltzes around the Officers' Club, until Mrs. Caconi snatches the newborn back, insisting he needs a bottle and a diaper change.

It's Mrs. Mattaman who notices Piper is nowhere to be found.

"Maybe she's still in the city," I suggest as Annie, Theresa, Natalie, and I sweep through the food line filling our napkins with cannolis, cookies, brownies, and cake.

"Go up to her house. All of you," Mrs. Mattaman insists, pushing us out into the foggy afternoon. "Make sure she's not holed up there all by her lonesome. Go on, you've got your marching orders, you hear?"

I'm not wild about this idea. Dealing with Piper these days is like picking up black widow spiders with my bare hands. But there's nothing else to do. Mrs. Mattaman is at the Officers' Club door, herding us up the hill. And Natalie is already ahead of us. I hurry and catch up.

The warden's house is dark and silent. It's as if the good news hasn't reached the top tier of the island yet. Not even Buddy and Willy One Arm are visible, though I can hear them working in the kitchen. The front door is partly open.

"Piper!" we call as Annie and I, Theresa and Natalie climb the stairs to Piper's room. Piper doesn't answer. The door to her room is closed. Annie knocks.

"What?" Piper barks.

"We brought you cookies," Annie tells her.

"I'm not hungry," Piper declares, opening the door. As we troop in, she snatches a cannoli out of my hand. For a second, I think she's going to toss it in the trash. Throwing away a Mattaman cannoli is like burning the American flag as far as I'm concerned. But no, she stuffs it in her mouth, squishing the cream out the back side.

"I'm *not* hungry," she mumbles, her mouth full of cream.

Theresa squints at her. "You should be happy now. Your mom is okay."

"What do you know about it?" she snaps, wiping her mouth with the back of her hand.

"My mom said she was better."

Piper nods. "She is better. I wish she'd come home," she admits as we hear Jimmy outside.

"Go get the door. It's Jimmy," Theresa commands.

"Why don't you get it?" Annie asks.

Theresa makes a face. "I don't like going down there by myself."

"Buddy Boy! Could you let Jimmy in!" Piper calls down.

Jimmy knocks another time.

"Buddy Boy!" Piper calls again.

Theresa jumps up and heads for the open hall window and pokes her head out. "That's not Jimmy. It's Mrs. Caconi."

"Sounded like Jimmy," Piper mutters.

Mrs. Caconi is inside now, climbing the stairs. "This is your own little house, Walter Williams. Not so little, either. Twenty-two rooms it is. Best one on the Rock." Mrs. Caconi is huffing and puffing harder than usual. She chuffs and hisses when she breathes, like a freight train.

Annie pokes me. "C'mon! We got to help her. She has trouble with stairs."

Mrs. Caconi is on the landing, leaning her heavy body against the banister and dabbing at her forehead. Her foot rocks the blue-ribboned basket with the tiny blanketed bundle, all wrinkly and red, no bigger than a banana bread. Hard to believe a person could ever be that small.

"Need some help, Mrs. Caconi?" I ask.

"Well, I wouldn't say no to a strapping young man like you carrying this baby up these stairs . . ."

"Yes, ma'am." I lift the basket, which is surprisingly light. Baby Rocky must weigh five times more than this little turnip. Annie stays with Mrs. Caconi as she slowly makes her way up the stairs.

"I'm not used to taking care of a newborn," Mrs. Caconi explains. "It's been umpteen years since my Donny was that small," she tells us as I plunk the basket on Piper's bed.

We all stare at the tiny baby, his eyes closed tight like a brand-new puppy's, a blue knitted beanie on his head.

"Been rocking him the last hour. I'm not as young as I once was you know." Mrs. Caconi sighs. " He's sleeping now, though. They're sweet as pie when they're sleeping, aren't they?"

"Baby," Nat mutters, her eyes whipping past the baby and past again as if they can't settle down for a full look. "Walter," Natalie whispers.

"It," Piper grunts. "His name is It."

"Oh now dear child, don't you start with that rubbish. I won't hear of it. No I won't. He'll grow on you, yes he will." Mrs. Caconi straightens the baby's beanie. "Your mama'll be home soon. And she won't tolerate that kind of talk."

Piper's eyes glaze over. "Thing," she whispers.

Mrs. Caconi ignores her. "Oh yes, indeedy. He had a big bottle and a nice clean diaper with me. Now you watch him while I catch forty winks, you hear me, little mMiss?" Mrs. Caconi points her handkerchief at Piper. "Fog's comin' in and it's dark as night. I'm gonna take a catnap before night shift. Little dickens woke up six times last night." She squints at Piper. "And don't you tell me no. Watching him while he's sleeping is not too tall an order for you. I should think not. You got a whole roomful of folks to help you here." She wags her finger at Piper and stumbles bleary-eyed into the next room.

No one says a word as she groans and grunts her way up on the big bed. In seconds she's snoring so loud it sounds like the foghorn next door.

Piper stares at the teeny tiny baby in his blue beanie cap. "Get *It* out of here," she whispers.

"Now you listen up," Theresa mimics Mrs. Caconi and wags her finger at Piper. "Taking care of babies is something I know all about." She taps her chest. "I'm going to teach you."

"Theresa!" Annie warns in a husky whisper.

Piper looks like she may hawk up a big one and spit it right at Theresa.

Theresa puts her hands on her hips. "Her mom's okay now. Do I still have to be nice to her?"

Piper gulps, then crumples into an exhausted heap.

"Uh-oh," Annie whispers. Her lips pucker up and her forehead wrinkles. She strokes Piper's hair. "We'll help, okay?" Annie nods to us and we all pipe in.

"Sure, we'll help," I say.

"Help. We'll help. Baby," Nat adds.

Annie smiles. "That's right, even Natalie will help."

Tears spill out of Piper's closed eyes. She pushes them away from her face in quick jerky motions. "I don't want a brother."

Natalie gets a tissue and wraps Piper's fingers around it, which only makes her cry harder.

We all stare at Piper. No one knows what to say. "Brothers aren't that bad," Theresa declares. "They squirt pee at you when you change their diapies, though, you gotta watch that." Theresa puts her finger down by her personal parts like it's a water hose. "They have their own private squirt gun."

"We have nothing of the kind," I insist.

"How would you know?"

"Because I know my own equipment. I'm pretty much an authority on it, okay?"

"Not when you were a baby."

"Moose! Piper!" Jimmy's voice again. This really is Jimmy.

"Buddy!" Piper calls again. "The door!"

Theresa pops up and checks the window. The fog is heavy and dark like a coat pulled tight around us. What time is it? "Don't the passmen have to go back to the cell house now?" Theresa asks.

"They go back at four thirty," Piper tells us. She has that fuzzy look, like someone who needs to sleep for two days straight.

Annie glances at her watch.

"I'll get him," I offer. Natalie gets up too. She has been amusing herself by tucking the baby's covers all around, then all around again. She is gentle with the baby. So gentle.

"Stay here, Nat. I'll be right back," I tell her softly.

Natalie chews at her lip. And Piper snaps to. "Wait, Moose. Moose! I'm coming down, too."

Theresa shakes her finger at Piper. "You can't. You have to watch the baby."

"Theresa," Annie warns.

"You have to take them everywhere with you, Piper. You can't just leave them." Theresa's chin juts out with the force of her words.

"You're going to be here. You watch her," Piper says in a

small voice.

"Well, what if I wasn't?" Theresa's hands are planted firmly on her hips. Her voice is full of authority. "This is training. *I* am training you. Remember what happened with me and Rocky? Do you want that to happen to *It*?"

"Theresa," Annie scolds. "Let Piper alone, okay?"

Piper stares hard at Theresa and then suddenly her face caves in. "Fine," she whispers, peering in at the baby. The baby's eyes are still closed. Piper glances anxiously at Annie. "The blanket too?" she whispers.

"Yep, you carry him in it," Annie explains.

Piper takes a deep breath, then wiggles her hands underneath the blanket, scooping the baby out of the basket. "I did it," she whispers, smiling a little. She carries him out the door, holding him away from her chest like a football.

"See, see what I did." Theresa pats herself proudly as I head for the door.

"Nat, really, you can stay."

"Nat home. I want to go home," Natalie says, stubbing her toe against the floor.

"Natalie, c'mon. Just stay here," I tell her.

"Nat home," she repeats.

"Okay," I concede. Natalie has been pretty cooperative today. I don't want to push it. "I'll send Jimmy up, then I'll take Nat home," I call back to Annie and Theresa.

"Why doesn't he just come in himself? Jimmy, c'mon," Theresa belts from Piper's room.

"Hey Jimmy!" I open the door into the now near blackness of the darkest September afternoon I've ever seen. Piper is right behind me, carrying her teeny tiny brother, followed by

Natalie.

"Light on, light on," Nat mutters. She snaps the switch at the front door back and forth, back and forth, but no light illuminates the gloomy outside.

"It's broken, Nat," I tell her.

The fog is blowing through like smoke. I can't even see the cell house, which is ten feet across the narrow Alcatraz road. The wind blows a tin can down the steep switchback. "Jimmy!" I shout. "They need my dad up here to fix these lights. Jim-meeeeee!"

Natalie walks behind me. She isn't touching me but her presence is close, too close. That's Natalie for you. She's always too close or too far away.

"He's not here. You go back. I'm going to take Nat home," I tell Piper, changing course under Piper's window, when suddenly something clammy and cold closes around my neck, crushing my throat.

"Shut it," a voice whispers in my ear, "or you die."

32. The Good Prisoner

****

Same day—Friday, September 13, 1935

"Don't say a word, not one word," Buddy Boy drawls.

It's only Buddy.

I breathe easier. Buddy won't let anything bad happen. Buddy likes us.

"Ease up." Willy One Arm's whiny voice.

The cold hand lessens its grip around my windpipe. I take a big breath and twist hard. The fingers burn into me like a taut rope. I can feel the tall hovering frame behind me, the whispery voice, the stale smell, and the three-fingered hand. It's Seven Fingers in a guard uniform complete down to his shiny black shoes.

Buddy Boy has one of Piper's hands twisted behind her back. Her other arm clutches the baby. Buddy Boy has a gun forced up into her back. Buddy? *Our* buddy.

He's dressed as a guard too. In front Willy One Arm, in a guard shirt and pants but no jacket, clutches Natalie in the crook of his one wiry arm. His gun is in his hand, covered by an undershirt. Nat's faced the other way as if she can't bear to look at Willy. Her head jerks in small agitated twitches, which startle Molly, who sits on Willy's shoulder.

"Quit it!" Willy whines. "Buddy! Make her stop."

"The warden's kid brought the baby." Seven Fingers's voice makes my skin crawl.

Natalie is shaking all over, trying to spin herself free of the arm around her throat, the gun jammed in her back. "Natalie doesn't like that. I don't I don't like that," Nat says.

Buddy smiles and smiles like he can't turn off his lips, but his eyes are like points on barbed wire. "What you bring the baby out for?" he growls at Piper.

"Just snap his neck." Seven Fingers's whispery Bull Durham breath in my ear.

"Buddy! Buddy! Tell him not to say that," I plead.

Willy One Arm tries to cross himself without loosening his grip on the still-twitching Natalie. "Can't do nothin' to that baby," he mutters.

I see a flash of the baby's eyes. He starts to cry.

Piper squirms like crazy, but Buddy has her tight. "Buddy, listen to me, Buddy." Piper's voice sounds sure and strong. "Don't do this. You're going to be in vaudeville, remember? You're good, Buddy. You are."

Buddy Boy slaps her head. "Shut it," Buddy says, his voice low and angry.

"I can cover for you." Piper's voice breaks. "If you let us go now."

Buddy whacks her again. "I said shut it!"

I lunge toward him, but Seven Fingers squeezes my neck with his arm and grinds the gun in my back.

The baby's cries are piercing now, as if he senses Piper's fear. "C'mon, Buddy," Piper wheedles. "We're friends, right?"

"Let me have that baby. I'll shut him up," Seven Fingers hisses.

"Can't kill a baby, Buddy!" Willy One Arm whines. "Not on the thirteenth."

Then I see something out of the corner of my eye. It's Jimmy, the real Jimmy coming up the back way. I need to get his attention. But how? I think about throwing a rock, but I can't get near one with Seven Fingers's arm around my neck. Besides, then Seven Fingers will see him. I have to do something quickly before he—but it's too late. Jimmy's already inside.

Will Annie and Theresa suspect something when we don't come back? No, I just said I was taking Natalie home. They'll figure Piper went down to 64 building with me.

"Take the baby, do something with him," Buddy Boy tells Willy One Arm. Buddy's arm snakes around Natalie, and Willy lets go. Natalie squirms like a wild thing. Buddy Boy cranks his arm tighter around her neck.

"Only got forty minutes till the next count," Seven Fingers hisses. "Not gonna blow my chances for a baby."

"Buddy! Buddy!" Willy One Arm whines, "I ain't no baby killer."

"All right," Buddy Boy hisses. "Go!"

Willy One Arm takes off, the baby in his arm, his running steps almost silent, his body low to the ground.

My brain is slow, skittering all over the place, adrenaline pumps through my body, making it hard to think. This is not a game. Buddy doesn't like us. He never did. That was his game.

He could kill Natalie. I have to think of something. And then slowly it occurs to me. Buddy did his Jimmy imitation. That lured us out here but now the real Jimmy is inside. If Buddy were to do a Jimmy imitation now, with Jimmy in the warden's house, wouldn't they suspect something odd is happening?

"I ain't stayin' here," Seven Fingers says.

"Willy's got the boatkey. You learn to swim all of a sudden?" Buddy Boy barks.

"What makes you think he's coming back?" Seven Fingers mutters.

"Where's he taking the baby?" Piper whispers.

No one answers her.

"Where . . . is. . . he . . . taking . . . the—" Piper repeats.

"Shut it." Seven Fingers tightens his grip on my neck.

"How'd you do that, Buddy?" I ask, my voice hoarse because of how tightly Seven Fingers is grasping my throat. "Make your voice sound like Jimmy?"

Buddy Boy flinches. "Shut up," he says in his Jimmy Mattaman voice.

But this wasn't loud enough for them to hear. "Yeah, but what did you say exactly?" I ask.

Buddy grunts like he's not going to do it. But I know Buddy. He can't resist showing off. "Moose! Piper!" Buddy imitates Jimmy a little more forcefully this time as Willy One Arm's dark, silent form comes slipping back to us. I want to look at the window in Piper's room to see if maybe I can spot Annie, Jimmy, or Theresa, but I don't dare.

"Let's go." Willy's out-of-breath whisper as he takes Natalie from Buddy and shoves her forward.

"Jimmy," Nat mutters. "Jimmy Mattaman."

"Get a move on." Seven Fingers's hot tobacco breath voice fills my ear. He kicks my calf.

"Three men, five arms. Five, five arms," Natalie mutters as the wind begins to howl.

"That's right, Nat." I make my voice as reassuring as possible.

She pitches a fit, they'll shoot her.

"Three men, five arms, no guns. No," Nat says.

Seven Fingers yanks my neck. "Shut … her … up!"

"*Shhh, shhh*, like in the library at home, Nat," I say in a panicky whisper.

"Zero," Nat mutters.

Seven Fingers crushed my windpipe. "Shut her up, I said."

"*Shhhh,*" Buddy Boy hisses, and Seven Fingers eases his hold just slightly as we tramp down the silent path by the parade grounds and around 64 building.

We're walking where guards are supposed to be. No hiding, no skulking, we're out in the open. Hiding in plain sight.

I try to think clearly about what is happening, but the gun in my back makes my mind slip and slide all around.

Buddy Boy impersonated Jimmy, hoping one of us would come out. They needed hostages. They weren't counting on Natalie and the baby. Their biggest problem now is time. At the 4:30 count the whole island will know they've escaped. What time is it now?

I have no idea. How can I slow them down?

I don't know that either.

It's so foggy we can hardly see. People can't see us either. Part of the reason they chose today to make a break. The other reason was the party. Nobody is thinking about the cons right now and they know it.

The cons have guns wrapped in shirts pointed in our backs. But they're walking close and holding them low. It doesn't look suspicious. Seven Fingers is whistling the same stupid tune Trixle always whistles. Willy One Arm has Mattaman's stiff-legged walk. Buddy has toothpicks in his mouth and my father's jiggy step. To all of Alcatraz it looks like a couple of families out for a stroll.

How close do you have to be to see this isn't my dad? In this fog, extremely close.

My heart beats so loud in my ears I can hardly think. We need to run into someone smart, but everyone smart is at the party.

There has to be a way out of this. The buck sergeant will know. He has to pull each card before we get on the boat. He'll see.

"Zero," Nat says again.

"Shut . . . her . . . up," Seven Fingers says with breathy, hate-filled pauses between his words.

"A little conversation"—my voice is so high and tight it doesn't even sound like mine—"is natural."

"Shut it," Buddy Boy says, but quieter this time, like he's agreeing with me.

I won one. For a second this calms me. Maybe I can win another. But what do I do? All I can think about is Nat's counting. She doesn't count nothing. She only counts something.

Zero. Zero what? *What has she been saying?*

Guns.

There are three guns. They each have one. I can feel Seven Fingers's gun in my back. Even Willy One Arm has an elbow around Nat's neck and a gun in his one hand. I try to get a better look at one of them in the dark, foggy afternoon. Buddy Boy has his gun pointed in Piper's back, but it's hidden. Why's he hiding the gun? In case someone walks by, he doesn't want them to see the gun, right?

If I can't see, how could Natalie see? How could she know

there aren't any guns?

She doesn't know.

I can't take Natalie's word for this. What am I crazy?

I try to get a better look at the gun in Nat's back, but she's behind me.

"Head forward." Seven Fingers grinds my heel.

This hurts but I can hardly feel it.

How could they get three guns?

What if they aren't guns? Wood could be shaped like a gun in the carpentry shop when a guard wasn't looking. Wood would get through the metal detector without setting it off.

But they have a key. A key is metal too. How'd they get that through the snitch box?

No guns. Zero.

The guard tower is above me. When we pass down by the dock, they have the best view of us. They've eased up on our throats now. If Mr. Mattaman thinks they're guards, he'll wave us on board. But he'll know. Of course he will. When I look up at the tower, I can barely see it. The fog is so thick, it has almost completely obscured the glass cage.

We're coming up to the boat. Buddy Boy does the wave. A perfect imitation of my father: the bent arm, the toothpicks in his mouth.

Where is the buck sergeant? The buck sergeant is always here. Mr. Mattaman, please stop us.

Mr. Mattaman doesn't stop us. How could he? He can't see.

We start across the gangplank. Once we're on the boat, Willy One Arm has the key. That is what Buddy was talking about. He won't have to wait for the buck sergeant to pull our cards. He won't have to wait for anything.

The gangplank sways. It's so foggy we can barely see the water right below us. I'm walking carefully, quietly, just as Seven Fingers and Buddy Boy want me to do. I'm a good prisoner. I'm doing everything exactly right.

It's safer just to go along, easier to do what they want me to do. Two steps on. Three. Four. Five. If I'm wrong, we could die.

But Natalie's never wrong. Not about counting. Not ever.

Why am I doing what they want?

"No!" I cry. My hand shoots up. I open my mouth and a voice booms out from the deepest part of my chest. "HELP!"

33. **OUTSIDE THE WARDEN'S HOUSE**

▪ ▪

Same day—Friday, September 13, 1935

Something cracks, a sound like splitting wood. The world spins, the boat deck is slipping out from under me. My legs buckle, a sharp pain rips my skull. But I try to hold on to myself. I can't lose consciousness. Can't go away. Nat needs me. Piper needs me.

The bright spotlight shines on us, blood floats out, warm blood I taste in my mouth.

The air is suddenly black with flies, swarms of them buzzing everywhere. Janet Trixle's voice booms through the bullhorn. "Stop!"

"They don't have guns!" I shout as loud as I can.

The second strike is harder. My knees buckle, the alarm bell blares, splitting my ears in two.

Then suddenly Seven Fingers is gone. I sway from the abrupt release of his hold on my neck. I try to keep from going down. Buddy Boy, Willy One Arm, and Seven Fingers scatter, leaping over us as the boat sputters to a start.

Out of the fog comes the clatter of Janet Trixle holding the bullhorn, running with Theresa. I hear the clip of something being thrown and then I see Annie tossing stones; one after the other she clobbers Seven Fingers right in the Adam's apple,

Buddy in the back. Guards are everywhere. More guards. Real guards. Rifle shots from the guard tower pelt the bay. Seven Fingers jumps the buck sergeant. Trixle thunders down the road waving his billy. Next thing I know Nat's shouting to Trixle, "No gun!"

Trixle squints at her, unsure whether to believe her or not.

"She's right. It's not a gun!" I shout as loud as I can and Darby vaults on Seven Fingers, who has the buck sergeant in a headlock. "Let go. Mother of God! Let go!" he shouts, his feet and arms pummeling Seven Fingers.

Seven Fingers lets go and Darby wrestles him to the ground, flattens him, holds his neck in a pincher grip.

The boat strains against the rope, bucking and roaring as Buddy Boy guns the engine, trying to pull the cleat out of the dock. Buddy Boy and Willy One Arm are barricaded in the captain's compartment. The boat roars, the dock creaks, Mr. Bomini jumps on top of the captain's compartment and bangs his billy, shattering the glass. Buddy Boy grabs Bomini's hand and tries to twist the billy out of it. More shots splatter down from the guard tower causing little explosions in the water. Annie pelts more stones. And then Buddy Boy comes out, waving a hummingbird handkerchief in the air, but hiding his head in his guard jacket, his smiling mouth finally still.

One Arm tries to bolt. He heads straight for the side of the boat like his plan is to jump overboard, but Bomini is too fast for him. He grabs him and slams him to the deck so hard, it knocks him out cold.

"C'mon," my father says, his arm around Natalie, pushing me, pulling Piper, back across the gangplank.

Tears stream down Nat's face. "No guns," she whispers.

My father's face is white as a flash of lightning in the dark sky as he herds Theresa and Janet, Jimmy and Annie, Piper and me into the canteen. Piper is ranting, her words slur. She grabs hold of my dad. "He's my brother. I have to find him."

"It's okay now, sweetheart." My father makes his voice as soft as fur, propping Piper up with his arm.

"You don't understand!" Piper shouts. "They took the baby!"

"What?" My father's neck snaps and then he sees me. "Moose, you're bleeding!" He's next to me now, his finger probing my head. He rips the sleeve of his shirt and dabs at the blood with it. "We got to get you to Doc Ollie."

"My brother!" Piper begs. She hangs on my father's jacket. "Please, please, *the baby*."

Janet Trixle still has the bullhorn and a look of stunned exhilaration on her face. She and Theresa are holding hands as they huddle together with Annie and Jimmy.

"I'm okay, Dad," I tell him, "but Willy took the baby."

"On the boat?"

"No, up top," I say.

Tears are streaming down Piper's face. "You have to help me."

My dad points to me. "Exactly where did you last see the baby?"

"Outside the warden's house."

"Willy One Arm took the baby," Nat echoes, flicking her chin against her chest. "One baby. Willy One Arm. One."

"Where?" My father's eyes are riveted to me.

"We don't know where!" Piper shouts.

My father nods a quick nod. "We'll send someone up there.

We'll find him." His voice is calm again, but his eyes dart toward
the phone outside Mrs. Caconi's door.

"I didn't, I didn't want him to," Piper whispers.

"Of course you didn't, honey. Of course not," my father
reassures her as he leaps outside to dial. "Officer Flanagan here.
The Williamses' baby is missing. Topside. Alcatraz #301. Willy
One Arm took her during the escape attempt. Last seen outside
the Williamses' house.

"What direction did he go?" My father leans in the door to
ask me.

"Toward the cell house," I say through the dull throbbing
of my head.

"North toward the cell house," my father reports into the
phone.

"Take me. I have to find him." Piper lunges toward my
father. She hangs on him as if her weight will sway him.

My father tries to unwind her hand from his arm. "Honey,
I think it's better if you—"

"NO," Piper shouts. "HE'S NOT YOUR BROTHER."

"Calm down," my father barks.

"Moose and I will go." Piper's voice is as tough as my
dad's.

"We'll all go," Annie suggests.

"We on lockdown?" my father asks into the phone.

"Annie, you stay put, you understand? You're in charge
down here," my father commands. And then into the receiver
he shouts: "Send the truck!"

A crowd has formed around us. "All residents, stay in your
apartments please. All residents," Bomini commands.

"Theresa, Jimmy, Annie, Janet, you stay right here, you

understand me?" My father's voice is so tough, I almost don't recognize it.

He looks at Piper. "You're going up top," he tells her. "Moose, I want Ollie to see your head. Nat, you're with me. We're going to go find your mom." He squeezes her hand—a quick squeeze, all that Nat can tolerate. "What a trooper you are," he whispers to her, his voice breaking.

"Natalie is a trooper," she repeats, her whole face glowing.

When the truck appears out of the smoky fog with Trixle in the driver's seat, we pile into the cab. The door shuts and my dad hops on the running board.

"Got the whole island looking for him now. We'll find him. Don't you worry," my dad tells Piper who is seated by the window. The truck lurches forward straining as it heaves up the steep hill.

When we get to the top, the warden is there. He wobbles toward the truck door, opens it with trembling hands, and Piper falls into his arms. "Oh my girl. My little girl." His voice is so choked, he can barely speak.

"The baby, Daddy," Piper cries. "The baby."

"Baby." Nat digs her chin deep down in her collarbone.

The warden nods, his eyes dazed like he can't quite figure out what is going on. "We'll find him," he says, but it doesn't sound as if he believes this.

He keeps his arm around Piper, holding her, protecting her, keeping her safe, as guards fan out all around, spilling out of everywhere. Searching. More guards than I even knew we had.

In the hustle and chaos, the sweep of the big spotlights from the guard tower, the bullhorn commands, I shadow my dad, sticking close like I'm a kid again. Mr. Bomini directs foot traffic and relays the warden's orders through his bullhorn. Doc Ollie is half running to the warden's house.

My father turns to me. "There's Ollie. Let's get you two inside," he says.

But when I look around, there is only me.

34. THE BOSS

Same day—Friday, September 13, 1935

"Natalie! She was just here," I tell my frantic father. My head is beginning to spin again.

"You go inside the wWarden's house. I shouldn't have had you out here in the first place."

"No!" I shout at him. "I can help! I know where she'll go."

He nods hesitantly. "Where?"

I try to pretend I'm Natalie. She wouldn't like the commotion. She'd go somewhere out of the noise.

My mind flashes on Nat in Piper's room. How gentle and careful she was with the baby. "Maybe she went to look for the baby?" I suggest.

"Where would she look?" my father asks.

"Around by the back of the cell house."

I head in the direction I saw Willy One Arm take the baby. I have no idea beyond this, but I don't want my dad to send me inside. I run as fast as I can, my father's thundering footsteps behind me.

I'm running like I know where I'm going, when all of a sudden out of the corner of my eye I think I see the flash of Nat's blue dress disappearing inside the hospital entrance of the cell house. Was that her? Could she have gone inside? This seems unlikely. My legs slow down.

"No way she could get in there." My father is sure about this.

I keep going.

"Moose!" my father calls.

I'm running now up the back stairs. "I think I saw her."

"Moose!" my father shouts. "Stop!"

The door is open. Down the corridor, past where a guard is conked out on the floor, I'm running all out, my feet pounding the floor. I can see Nat in her blue dress standing in the corridor.

"Natalie!" my father shouts.

Piper's little brother—the tiny baby—he's here. Capone has him in his arms.

"Baby," Nat says, looking toward Capone's cell. Oh my god, the baby's neck is broken, snapped in two by the raw power of Al Capone.

But the baby is sleeping. He has his eyes closed, snuggled up in the crook of Al Capone's arm. He is rocking him gently, ever so gently.

Nat is outside Capone's hospital cell. Capone is inside with the baby. The door is locked. How did the baby get in there?

My father stops. His eyes dart between Capone, the baby, and Natalie, taking it all in.

"Lost something, boss?" Capone whispers.

"Don't hurt him." My father's voice shakes with quiet power. He could command the entire Western Hemisphere with that voice.

"I'm not gonna hurt him. Been rocking him for close to an hour now."

"How'd he get in there?" my father asks.

"Molly," Nat whispers, pointing to the tiny mouse sitting on Capone's bed.

"Natalie followed the mouse." Capone smiles. "Smart girl you have there, boss. The mouse took off—went to find some food, I guess. But she came back. Took a liking to me. Everybody likes Uncle Al."

"The baby," my father says. "How'd the baby get in there?"

Capone smiles, a sly smile. "Moose, pull that bar. That one there." Capone directs me to the bar with his chin. "Slip it out real gentle and the next one over too."

I grab hold of the bar he means. As soon as I do I feel the give as a two-foot section pulls out in my hand. My father pulls out the next bar over and I get the last one. A neat square appears: just chest size—big enough for a man to crawl through.

Capone nods. "You got it, boss." He stands up, still rocking the tiny baby. Carefully he hands the little bundle through the opening to my father, tucking in his blanket under my father's arm.

"What in the H.?" my father mutters, cuddling the baby more awkwardly than Capone. The baby begins to cry.

"Just doing a bit of baby-sittin' is all."

Little Walt is starting to fuss now, twisting his small head.

"Rock him a little, why don't you?" Al suggests, eyeing the tiny baby whose face is growing redder in the half-light.

My father ignores this. "How'd the bars get cut?"

"Ain't tool-proof up here. You know that."

"Who did this?"

"I didn't do nothing. But I might have seen somebody working on 'em with dental floss and cleanser. Dental floss and cleanser cut anything. Did you know that?"

"*Might have seen?*" my father asks as the baby continues to fuss.

"Been a lot of activity here tonight. Case you missed it. Hard to know where to focus your eyes is all."

"You'll have to do better than that."

Capone coughs. He looks my father straight in the eye. "Only got three more years. And I got my own son. What's his mama gonna tell him—I pull a stupid stunt, get myself locked up for the rest of my life. I know a cockamamie plan when I hear one, but I'm no rat."

"That's not going to cut it, Al."

Capone looks down at the baby my dad is holding. "He was sleepin' with me. He's squallin' with you, boss."

"Who was involved?"

"Didn't see no one up close. My eyesight ain't so good anymore," Capone tells my dad.

"What in the name of Peter and Paul!" Trixle's boots pound down the aisle.

"Beats the life out of me, Darby," my father tells him.

"A trooper. I am a trooper," Nat tells Trixle proudly.

Trixle squints. "What's she saying?"

"*She* found the baby," I tell Trixle.

"Ain't possible."

"She sure did, Darby," my father murmurs, glowing at Nat.

"I'll be gar darned. She's the one told me they didn't have

guns too." Trixle looks at Nat, a flash of surprise in his eyes before he turns his attention to Capone. "Bars cut?" Trixle asks.

"Yep," my father says.

"Baby's okay?"

"Seems fine," my father answers.

"Rock him a little, will ya?" Al says. "Don't like to hear him squallin' that way."

"What happened, 85?" Trixle asks.

"Didn't see much, Officer. Busy as I was baby-sittin' and all."

Trixle eyes the opening. "I'll get the key. Can't stay in that cell."

"Don't see why not. If I was gonna leave, don't you think I'd have hightailed it out of here already?" Capone asks.

My father ignores him.

"Isn't that right, Moose?" Capone nods to me.

"Don't talk to him!" my father barks.

"Ahh, boss. He's a good boy, your Moose. I wouldn't go getting in the way of that, now would I?" Capone's eyes are hard, challenging my dad.

Trixle comes back with the key. The door clanks clean open again. "Had enough of your shenanigans tonight, 85. Put you in the Hole. That ought to help your eyesight some. Gonna be twenty-twenty when I'm done with you."

"The Hole?" Capone raises his hands. "That ain't fair. I been baby-sittin' the warden's baby. Should be getting' good time for this," he shouts as we walk out.

My father shakes his head. "Not sure what you do with a

guy like that. He does good things. But then he goes and does bad things right over the top of them," my father says as he tucks the blanket around Piper's little brother. "Now come on, let's get you home where you belong."

35. THE PIXIE JAILER PLAYGROUND

■ ■

Thursday, September 19, 1935

Right after the escape attempt, there is a euphoria that envelops the island. Everyone from Warden Williams to Darby Trixle is amazed by what seven kids were able to do all on our own. No one can get enough of the story, demanding we tell our version of events again and again.

My parents are practically bursting with pride because of what I did and because of Natalie. Not only did Natalie understand exactly what was going on, but she figured out something I hadn't. This very fact has given us hope we didn't have before. Natalie is getting better. Maybe not in the dramatic way my mom thinks she is . . . but better for Natalie.

How did it happen that three convicts came so close to escaping from the world's most secure prison? Slowly some of the pieces begin to fall in place. Mae delivered the boat keys to the island wrapped in her handkerchief. A convict swept them up with his push broom and slipped them in his pocket. The keys probably came from an officer on Angel Island. Our boat, the *Coxe* is owned by the army, and someone on Angel Island has a key.

Capone helped out his hospital cellmate Seven Fingers, but he did not try to escape. He was smart enough to know the escape was ill conceived. He wanted no trouble with the guards who have the power to extend his sentence or with the cons who would kill him if he didn't contribute to the escape. He got Mae to bring in the keys to the boat. He played his banjo every night to mask the sound of Seven Fingers sawing the bars with his floss. And he conveniently got behind in his guard shoe-shine service, so he had two pairs of guard shoes in his cell: one for Buddy and one for Seven Fingers. One Arm wore the warden's shoes, which were three sizes too large.

Each morning we wake up and find out something else. We still don't know how Seven Fingers got out of the cell house. No one knows how he got that key. My dad says we may never know.

It all seems so exciting and then one day . . . it isn't.

That's the day we find out the warden thinks the cons had help from the inside. The escape, he says, could not have happened without the aid of one of us.

Then my father, Associate Warden Chudley, Trixle, Mattaman, Bomini, and every other officer not on duty is called to the warden's office for a meeting that lasts all day and on until the wee hours of the night. One by one and in groups every man on the island is personally grilled by the warden. More meetings go on for days, and when my dad comes home each night, his toothpick box is empty and the deep furrows down the sides of his mouth are back.

He and my mother close the door of their room and whisper well into the morning. I go into Nat's room, stand outside their door, even sneak into the secret passageway, but all I hear is muffled mumbles.

No one knows what's happening now. Natalie, who was

supposed to return to the Esther P. Marinoff School the night after the escape, is still with us. And when I ask my mom why Nat hasn't returned to school, she evades my question with a tightlipped smile, giving no inkling of what's going on.

Finally, when I can stand it no longer, my father agrees to talk. There's some debate about whether Natalie should be included in the discussion, but in the end my dad decides that Natalie has earned this right. She's allowed to sit in her favorite spot on the floor, flipping the pages of her books. It's as if Natalie has earned a place in our family she didn't have before.

My father paces. He picks up his box of toothpicks from the coffee table and moves it to the kitchen table, then moves it back.

I look from my mom to my dad, wondering why they are so upset. "We're not going to be kicked off the island, are we?" I ask.

"No," my father answers, his eyes watchful.

"What did the warden say?"

"What can he say? The pass men worked at his house. It was his idea to throw that party and invite all of his best men. There's plenty of blame to go around."

"What about Natalie? Is he mad at her?"

"How can he be mad at her? She found his baby son. Even Trixle gave Natalie credit for letting him know Seven Fingers was unarmed. Course, Darby being Darby, he waxed eloquent on the need for a full report to J. Edgar Hoover, until Mattaman pointed out that right now in his own living room was a bar spreader being used as a carnival pole."

"It's the centerpiece of Janet's pixie merry-go-round."

"So I've heard. Janet says she found it on The b Bar spreader is made of steel. It would sink like a stone for one thing."

"Do they think Trixle had something to do with the escape?"

My father shrugs. "It hasn't been ruled out."

I think about how much I hate Trixle. How he tries to trip me up whenever he can. How awful he is to Natalie. How sick I felt when he talked about how he treated his brother. If I open my mouth, I'm putting Natalie in jeopardy. But I wasn't brought up to let someone else take the blame for something he didn't do, even if it is a nitwit like Darby Trixle.

"The bar spreader was in Natalie's suitcase," I tell my father. "Jimmy threw it in the bay, but he can't throw to save his life, so it didn't go very far. Janet Trixle found it and decided to use it for her pixie ponies. She had no idea what it was."

"Natalie? Natalie's involved in this?" My mom's voice is wrung tight.

My father gulps as if he swallowed one of his toothpicks.

"Yes," I whisper.

"Bottom drawer," Natalie murmurs, pulling at her dress like it's bothering her.

My father ignores this. His attention is riveted on me. "How did it get in her suitcase?"

I shake my head. "I dunno."

My father frowns, trying to see inside me. "You don't know?"

The question hangs between us. He clearly thinks I know more, but I've told him the truth. I have no idea how the bar spreader got there.

"Moose, remember when you had that nightmare about 105? Was that after you found the bar spreader?"

"Yes," I whisper, focusing my attention on my baseball bat, which is leaning against the door to my room.

"And that's when the metal detector went off? And Riv thought it was because of the metal buttons."

"Yes."

My father looks at my mother. My mother nods a tiny nod like he should go on. "That fits," he says., "But why did you suspect 105? That's the part I don't understand."

"I just did."

"You just did?" My father's voice has a hot edge.

I study the pattern on the carpet. "I think he . . . 105, he, um . . ." I'm breathing hard like saying these words requires more lung power than I possess. ". . . liked her," I mutter as the memory of 105 holding hands with Natalie comes flooding back.

My mom and dad stare at each other, their faces washed gray in the dusk. My mom nods to my dad as if to signal him to go on.

My dad takes a deep breath. "You were right to worry about 105," he says. "Sadie called us a few days ago. She said that Johnny Jay, Alcatraz 105, aka Onion, worked as a gardener at the Esther P. Marinoff School for a few weeks and then he disappeared. Apparently, he faked his references and they didn't know his background. They only found out because they discovered a letter he wrote to Natalie."

I swallow a big gulp of air. "A letter? He wrote her a letter?"

My father bites his lip. "Yes."

"What kind of a letter?"

He groans, stares out the window at the guard tower. "A

love letter," he whispers.

I look at Nat who is concentrating on her button box. She has taken all of her buttons out and she's putting them back in a new order.

"The letter said 105 loves her?" I ask.

My father makes a clicking noise. "It was a goodbye love letter, isn't that right, Helen? It said he was going back home to Portland for good."

"Everyone at the Esther P. Marinoff knows who he is now," my mom whispers. "They aren't going to let him anywhere near Natalie."

"The man lied about his references. Can't blame him for that. Hard enough to get a job with half the country out of work. It's impossible if you've got a record." My dad shakes his head. "It's not going to be easy to prove he put a bar spreader in Natalie's suitcase."

"We won't need to prove that. We won't be prosecuting," my mother snaps.

My father splits a toothpick in two. "Of course we will, Helen."

"Over my dead body." My mother's voice has gone cold as a cadaver. "The papers get a hold of this and what do you think will happen? Think this through, Cam."

"*Crazy Daughter of Alcatraz Guard Aids Escape*," I say, "but the cons never got the bar spreader. Natalie didn't help the cons to escape, she helped stop them from escaping."

"I know what she did. You know what she did," my mother says. "But what will some reporter who wants a sensational story make of it? We can't have that much attention focused on Natalie. The warden will kick us out of here. He'll have no choice."

My father shakes his head. "Why didn't you tell us about this, Moose?"

"Same reason we didn't tell *him*, Cam," my mom whispers. "He was protecting us, just like we were protecting him."

"He should have told us." My father sighs. "Nobody can do this all alone. Nobody has all the pieces. We need each other."

"And what if Moose had told you? You would have run up to the warden in a heartbeat. We'd be off the island with no means of support and no way to pay for the Esther P. Marinoff School. You think Moose doesn't know all that?" My mom is on the edge of her seat. Her chest is heaving from the force of her words.

"It wasn't the right thing to do," my father insists.

"In a perfect world you'd be right," my mom answers.

"Helen, come on. Look what happened here. The whole place fell apart."

"The bar spreader didn't cause that. The bar spreader didn't do anything but prop up a seven-year-old's pretend ponies," my mom tells him.

"Okay," my father says, "but it could have. We got lucky is all."

My mom leans in, her pupils so large they take over the brown of her eyes. "Maybe we did, but like you said there's enough blame to go around here, Cam. The warden is going to dig the deepest hole he can and bury this. He's going to see the light just like Trixle did. Do you think he wants to give a report to J. Edgar Hoover that says everything fell apart while he was throwing a party? The only people who really were on top of the situation were *kids*. Can you imagine those headlines?"

"*Kids Apprehend Escaping Prisoners,*" I say.

"The kids. We kids. We," Natalie mutters like she's practicing for Sadie.

"We need to tell the warden about this, Helen." My father's voice is calm but deadly firm.

"We will do no such thing," my mother answers.

"Helen." My father's eyes bore a hole into her. "I can't live this way. We will tell the warden and we'll see what happens. But you're probably correct," he concedes. "So long as the press doesn't get wind of it, the warden will most likely let this go."

My mom doesn't answer, but I think she knows she's lost this one. Her silence is consent.

"And from now on I want to know what's going on, you understand?" My father points a toothpick at me.

"Natalie caused problem. Natalie. I caused problems," Nat mutters.

"No you didn't, sweet pea," my dad tells her, "You made me proud and don't you forget it."

"I am a trooper," Nat whispers. "I am. Me."

My father walks over to where I'm sitting with Natalie. He pats my shoulder awkwardly and gently touches her hair. "We're a family of troopers. We'll get through this, Helen, the same way we always do . . . by doing the right thing."

36. KIDS ON THE ROCK

■ ■

Sunday, September 22, 1935

Eventually things settle down. Whether this is because of the talk my father has with the warden or not, I really don't know. But the sudden fear that hit our island disappears and everything goes back to the way it was—almost everything anyway. Asociate Warden Chudley is demoted. The warden finally realized what my dad and everyone else had known for some time. He was not up to his job.

But the biggest change as far as I'm concerned occurs among us kids. What happened when the cons tried to escape changed the way we think about each other. Each of us contributed something important that dark afternoon. Janet saw Theresa running down from up top and she came out with her bullhorn. Theresa found out she'd been right about the importance of Mae's hummingbird hanky. Jimmy figured out what was going on and snuck down under the dock to set loose his flies to swarm the cons at exactly the right moment. Natalie's attention to detail helped her spot the fake guns and let me know about them in her own unique way. Annie made use of that perfect pitching arm. And Piper discovered that deep down inside she might just have it in her to love her baby brother.

But it wasn't just that. It was what Mrs. Mattaman said

too . . . about how everybody disappoints you at one time or another and you have to forgive people. That seemed to make a difference too.

At the parade grounds today, Annie throws the first pitch and we all find our places. Jimmy is catcher. He still can't throw to save his life, but he taught himself to catch pretty well—not bad at all. Theresa is shortstop and I'm on first base. Janet Trixle is up at bat and Natalie is the ump calling the pitches, which she does with machine-like accuracy. And of course Annie chucks her perfect pitches over the base one after another.

Not surprisingly, Piper isn't here . . . some things never change.

After we're done playing, Jimmy and Annie and I are walking back down to 64 building when I tell Jimmy it's too bad he had to let all his flies go and he says, "You don't care about flies."

"Yes, I do," I insist.

"You try to, but that's different." He nods toward Annie. "Annie's never liked the flies, but she told me right at the start. It's easier that way. This island is too small for pretending."

I feel the slap in his words and I really want to tell him he's wrong, but he's not. "Sorry, Jim," I say.

He shrugs, takes his glasses off, and cleans them on the tail of his shirt. "We're all sorry about something," he says.

"What are you sorry about?" I ask hopefully. I hate to be the only guy who messed up.

"Telling Scout about the secret passageway."

"Yeah, why'd you do that anyway?"

Jimmy shrugs and rubs his glasses harder. "I thought you

were going to tell Scout yourself, I wanted to beat you to the punch. And I was hoping Scout's opinion of me would . . .you know."

"Rise above the status of dead girl?" I ask.

He grins into his glasses.

"I'm not sure which is worse, dead girl or auntie," Annie complains, shifting her baseball pants the way a guy would.

"Okey-dokey is what I said," I tell her.

"This is supposed to make me feel better?" Annie snaps. "Not that I care. I've never been sweet on you, Moose. I've always thought you were a slug."

"Well thank you," I say, looking out across the bay where a flock of pelicans are flying in awkward formation.

"You're welcome." She smiles a little. "I have no idea why my mother would say that. It couldn't be further from the truth."

"No offense, Annie, but your mom has some nutty ideas. She and her

needlepoint . . ." I tell her.

Annie snorts. "Moose, Moose, Moose, don't get me started on that. My mom thinks you *love* needlepoint."

"It's hard to tell when he likes something and when he doesn't," Jimmy grumbles.

I wish Jimmy would let up on this.

Annie's big lips pucker like she's thinking about this. "But that's what we like about him too, isn't it?" Annie looks past me to Jimmy. "That he tries so hard with everyone."

I'm glad Annie has said this. I am just being nice. What's the matter with that? But then I remember walking onto the boat with Seven Fingers's arm choking my throat, One Arm marching Natalie across, Buddy dragging Piper.

People say I was heroic by calling for help the way I did, but I know how close I came to staying silent.

I scared myself that night. I saw how much I want to get along. But sometimes you have to make trouble. Sometimes making trouble is the right thing to do.

Life is complicated. You'd think on a prison island—what with the bars and the rules and everything—it would all be so clear . . . but it's not.

. . . .

Monday, September 23, 1935

Nat's going back to the Esther P. Marinoff School today. She hasn't pitched a fit about it either. Of course my mom has made sure her yellow dress is brand-new clean—the one with the buttons Sadie sews on every time she's done something well. My mom is in the kitchen packing up the lemon cake to take along, just in case Trixle decides to sharpshoot into the bay like the last time. Even though Trixle admitted Natalie helped apprehend the cons, he still isn't her biggest fan. I don't think there's anything Natalie could do to change his mind about that either. Trixle's mind is made of stone. It doesn't change; it just chips off here and there.

Nat is smiling to herself and running her hands along the buttons on her yellow dress.

"Good idea Sadie had there. Kind of like badges the generals wear," I tell her, surveying the small collection of buttons on Nat's dress. They look like they belong on the dress because Sadie has sewn them so artfully.

"New button." Nat runs her fingers along the bottom button, which is small and ordinary—the kind sewn on a man's shirt. But when it comes to buttons there's no such thing as ordinary for Natalie. It's like me and baseball games, I guess. No two are alike.

"I'll bet Sadie will give you a new button if you cooperate today," I tell Natalie.

Nat shakes her head emphatically as if she wants to jiggle the hair right out of her scalp. "New button." She points again to the simple white button.

"Not that new. You haven't seen Sadie in two weeks, you know," I tell her.

"No Sadie."

"No Sadie. Mom put that on?"

"No Mom."

"Dad?" My voice squeaks hopefully, though I can't imagine Dad threading a needle, much less sewing a button on.

"No Dad." Natalie keeps shaking her head. "Moose."

"I didn't sew it on, Natalie. Mom's just kidding about me sewing."

"No Moose," Natalie agrees.

"Who did it then?" I ask.

"Good job," Nat answers, handing me a scrap of paper—brown with lines folded in half in handwriting I've come to know so well.

Good job, it says.

Author's Note

■ ■

Alcatraz Island . . . What Really Happened?

Al Capone Shines My Shoes is a novel, grounded in history, but heavily embroidered by my imagination. While the characters of this book and the actions they take are completely fictional, some of the scenes came from true stories.

It was true, for example, that the families of most Alcatraz guards lived on the island during the years Alcatraz was a working penitentiary. Jolene Babyak described her experience living on Alcatraz this way: "Alcatraz was like a small town with one bad neighborhood. Children played baseball, flew kites and played 'guards and cons' under the shadow of the cell house."[1]

The year 1935 was in the midst of the Depression. Money was scarce. Convicts who had trade skills worked for free as plumbers and electricians, painters, movers, custodians, gardeners, and trash collectors in the "civilian"—as the families on the island were sometimes called—homes and apartments.

Jimmy and Moose's dilemma about how to dispose of the bar spreader came from a true fact of island life. Since the convicts acted as trash men, island residents had to be careful about what they tossed out. As one island resident remembers: "No glass, razor blades or other sharp objects in our garbage as prisoners were detailed to pick it up."[2]

The convicts did the laundry for everyone who lived on the island. Though note-passing through the laundry was a figment of my imagination, the laundry sometimes did provide a vehicle for convicts to let hated guards know how they felt. Rocky Chandler, who grew up on Alcatraz in the thirties, described the phenomenon this way: "Convicts had their own small ways of hassling. Because the wind was cold up on the tower catwalks, most guards wore long john underwear beneath their uniforms. Occasionally EF Chandler's underwear would come from the laundry starched stiffer than a board."[3] There were other island families who refused this service as the laundry often "came back mangled."[4]

Convicts on special detail were accompanied by a guard, but human nature being what it is, rules were occasionally relaxed or even broken. Surprising alliances formed in the most unlikely of circumstances. George DeVicenzi, a guard from 1950 to 1957, told me one of the most feared convicts on Alcatraz, Jimmy Groves, came to his aid one night when he had night duty in the cell house. Night duty was long and tedious at best, terrifying at worst, and one boring evening George fell asleep at his desk. He was awakened by Jimmy throwing crumpled-up sheets of paper at him from his second-tier cell. Groves, who had a bird's-eye view of the cell house corridor, saw George's supervisor approaching and he didn't want George to be written up for falling asleep on the job.[5]

There were plenty of stories of Alcatraz children breaking the rules as well. As one boy who grew up on Alcatraz put it: "[I could] probably write several pages of things Phil Bergen [captain of the guards] caught me doing."[6] Or as Chuck

Stucker said: "Two-thirds of the island was restricted, what do you think a boy was going to do? Go to the places he's not supposed to."[7]

Still, there was a stiff penalty for misbehaving. As Bob Orr, who lived on the island from 1941 to 1956, said: "We couldn't mess up, violate rules or we'd be asked to leave the island."

Ed Faulk, a resident on the island in the thirties, told me he came home one day from school to his father and three convicts sitting around his kitchen table. Sharon Haller said the parents of her friends in San Francisco sometimes would refuse to let their kids visit her on Alcatraz because they thought "we ate dinner with the convicts." But they did not. Ed Faulk's story is the only evidence I have found of the convicts sitting down at the same table with the civilians.

But for the guards—the fathers of the children who lived on the island—there was a terrifying side to life on the island. As one former resident described it: "The danger was there. Everyone knew. All you have to do is take the bone out of a T-bone steak and you've got an excellent weapon."[8] During the escape attempt in 1946 known as the Battle of Alcatraz, two guards were killed—both family men.

And sometimes the convicts did know more about the families who lived on the island than they had any right to know. Chuck Stucker told me about his return to the island after having been gone for eight years. As soon as he got off the boat, one of the convicts on dock duty tapped him on the shoulder and asked, "Are you Ed Stucker's son? Tell your father hello. I always liked that man."[9]

Perhaps the most peculiar fact of life on the island involved the convicts who worked in the warden's home. "The wardens all employed exemplary prisoners known as 'passmen' to cook and clean at the residence, and every thirty minutes these inmates would emerge onto the front porch, where they would stand until they had been counted by an officer who could see them through a prison administration window."[10]

And yes, some of the wardens had school-age children living on the Rock. James A. Johnston, the first warden on Alcatraz, had a daughter named Barbara who described what happened when her mother, Ida Mae Johnston, came upon the two passmen fighting in her kitchen. Apparently Ida shook her finger at the men and said: "You boys. You stop that right now." And they did.[11]

Generally the passmen were selected because they had relatively short sentences, thus they were not considered flight risks. But there is evidence that more than one passman took advantage of his situation. A houseboy and a cook were said to have a still in the warden's basement from which they made a home-brewed wine out of fermented fruit.

Bill Dolby, who lived on Alcatraz as a boy and had the job of delivering newspapers on the island, remembered his interactions with the warden's passman, Chief Wareagle. "Carrying the newspapers gave me access topside and to the lighthouse. Chief Wareagle met me every morning to take the paper and slip me some freshly made cookies or candy. After a while I told [the chief] not to do that any more because I didn't want to get Dad in trouble . . . which was difficult to do since he made really good pralines."[12]

Clifford Fish, a guard on Alcatraz for twenty-four years,

talked about a passman named Montgomery who, because of his unique ability to come and go from the cell house, was asked to participate in the 1946 escape attempt. Montgomery decided against involvement because he "had too good of a job (on Alcatraz)." But neither did he forewarn guards of the impending escape because if he had he would have been killed by the other convicts.[13]

The prison was, after all, a maximum security operation that housed some of "the world's most dangerous criminals."[14] You did not typically go directly to Alcatraz. "To qualify for a reservation at Alcatraz, the tough customers must have demonstrated their incorrigibility at the other prisons or . . . [be suspected] of running rackets or gangs from within prison walls."[15] In 1935, you were sent to Alcatraz if you were a troublemaker at another prison or an "accomplished escape artist."[16]

The reason Al Capone was moved from the Cook County facility in Illinois to Atlanta and then to Alcatraz was because he worked the prison system to his own advantage. In Cook County he was able to bribe, or "tip," as he preferred to call it, the guards and live the high life behind bars. "It was said he convinced many guards to work for him, and his cell boasted expensive furnishings including personal bedding . . . [the cell was] carpeted, and he had a radio around which many of the guards would sit with him conversing and listening to their favorite serials."[17] In fact, "a clue to his power [in prison] could be found in a recess carved in his tennis racket's handle. He might have a couple of thousand dollars secreted there at any given time."[18]

Warden Johnston described Capone this way: "He was suave and aggressive by turns, and it was apparent from the beginning that he was trying to show the other prisoners that he would find some way to get what he wanted inside, just as he had always got what he wanted when he was outside."[19]

Capone's challenge on Alcatraz was avoiding trouble from the other inmates. At one point Capone's empire was worth $62 million[20] (more than $950 million in today's dollars), and some inmates wanted him to bankroll their escape. "Upon arriving at the Island Al was approached . . . to advance $5000 to be used as an escape plan to hire a gun-boat."[21] In 1936 a young punk named Jimmy Lucas stabbed Capone with a pair of barber scissors. Lucas's motivation was simply to prove that he—and not Capone—was the toughest guy on Alcatraz.

Capone, though a ruthless and vile human being, was not without his charming side. As Phyllis (Hess) Twinney, the daughter of the first doctor on Alcatraz explained it to me: "Dad liked Al. But Dad was under no illusions about Al, who thought everyone was his servant.

"Even so, Al saved Dad's life. Dad had to take visiting hours. The con ahead of Al came in and got really agitated. Every doctor had a little scalpel so he could lance something if needed. The guy went ballistic, grabbed up the scalpel, and came toward my father. Al heard the commotion. Al was very soft-footed for a big man, and he inched his way in, grabbed him from behind, and shook the scalpel from his hand."[22]

Although Warden Johnston tried to treat him as if he were no different from other convicts, in some small ways his infamy did penetrate the thick walls of Alcatraz. Many guards, as the story goes, gave Al their hats for him to dust off so they could brag, "Al Capone dusted off my hat."[23] But so far as I know, Al Capone didn't shine guards' shoes. However, he did work at the shoe shop in his previous prison in Atlanta, so it is likely he was an accomplished shoe shiner.

Al Capone never worked as a waiter on Alcatraz either, but the Officers' Club sometimes employed convicts as waiters, and there is anecdotal evidence of convicts spitting or placing broken glass in a hated guard's food.

Unless you were a friend of an Alcatraz civilian, it was practically impossible to gain access to Alcatraz. VIPs and celebrities, however, were given tours on a regular basis and the administration might very well put on the dog for such visits.

There is one photo that documents a visit of J. Edgar Hoover to Alcatraz, but it's likely he visited more than once as creating a maximum security prison on Alcatraz was his brainchild. Eliot Ness was never, to my knowledge, on the island, so his inclusion in that scene was entirely fictional. Mae Capone was a frequent visitor to the island, and if the press got wind of a visit, reporters mobbed her at the Fort Mason dock where she boarded the ferry for Alcatraz.

The story of Willy One Arm picking the pocket of J. Edgar Hoover is fictional. It's highly unlikely such a ploy would ever have been pulled on the head of the FBI, but the idea for that scene came from an incident relayed by Clifford Fish. According to Fish, Associate Warden Miller liked to pull that routine on visiting dignitaries. He used a convict by the name of Pivaroff, a pickpocket or "dip," as it was sometimes called.

Miller would give the nod to Pivaroff once he decided who would be the mark, and Pivaroff would pick his pocket. Then Miller would hand the visiting VIP his wallet and say, "You just had your pocket picked on Alcatraz."[24]

And strangely enough, movies were shown to the convicts on Alcatraz once a month. The favorite movie star of many of the Alcatraz inmates in the late thirties and early forties? Shirley Temple.

Although no escape exactly like the one depicted in *Al Capone Shines My Shoes* was ever tried, many of the details are based on other escape attempts. One convict escaped by impersonating an officer—though he only got as far as neighboring Angel Island before he was caught. Another convict smuggled a bar spreader into the cell house inside his steel guitar. The flat soft prison bars in the Hole (like those in the hospital) were cut in that same escape attempt. An abrasive cleanser and dental floss could be used for this—and, yes, dental floss did exist in 1935.[25]

Some convicts also befriended mice. "Hungry for companionship, some inmates made pets out of mice they found in their cells. They made nests in their bathrobe pockets..."[26] In another account, one inmate kept his mouse in his shirt pocket and surreptitiously fed him food crumbs when the officers weren't looking.

After having connected directly to more than twenty people who lived on the Rock during the penitentiary years, the one sentiment that seemed to come through in each person's story was what a close-knit group this was. As one man who lived on the island as a boy put it: "[Living on Alcatraz was like] having a lot of uncles everywhere to watch over us."[27] Or as Phyllis Twinney said when I asked her if she'd ever thought of running away from Alcatraz: "Why would anyone run away from Alcatraz? It was home."

More About Natalie

Like Moose, Piper, Annie, Scout, and the other kids in this book, Natalie is a fictional character. I did borrow some of the behaviors and perhaps a little of the essence of my own sister, Gina Johnson, in building Natalie's character. Gina was diagnosed with classic autism at the age of five.

If Natalie were a real person alive today, she would probably also be diagnosed somewhere on the autism spectrum. But since autism had not been identified in 1935, I could not use that word in this novel.

Though I do have a personal connection to autism, I did not set out to write a book containing a character with autism. When I got the idea to write about Alcatraz, I signed up to be a docent on the island. During the year I was an Alcatraz volunteer, I found myself thinking a lot about Gina. The island reminded me of her. Alcatraz is a lonely block of concrete plunked down in the middle of the spectacular San Francisco Bay, close enough to see the glittering city lights but set apart forever and always—a prison in paradise. Gina was beautiful and oddly perceptive but separated from the rest of us, locked in her own tormented world. When Gina was eight, she drew a picture of a stick figure in a prisonlike box and said, "This is Gina."

Though we still know surprisingly little about what causes autism, the treatment options have improved dramatically in the last fifteen years. The possibility of partial or even complete recovery from autism is greater now than it was when my sister was a kid. The chances of a life rich in its own rewards, for children on the autism spectrum is much more likely today. For Gina, who died when she was eighteen, autism was a prison without a key. I like to think I've given my sister's spirit a new life in the pages of these books.

NOTES

1 JOLENE BABYAK, quote displayed on Alcatraz Island in cell house (2007).

2 ERIN CRAIG lived on Alcatraz Island from 1947–1949. Letter to Alcatraz Alumni Association President Chuck Stucker.

3 ROY CHANDLER AND E. F. CHANDLER, *Alcatraz: The Hardest Years: 1934–1938* (Jacksonville, N.C., Iron Brigade Armory Publishers, 1989), 127.

4 SHARON HALLER lived on Alcatraz Island from 1960–1963. Speech about living on Alcatraz given at the Astoria Public Library, Astoria, Ore, on March 13, 2008.

5 GEORGE DEVICENZI lived and worked on Alcatraz Island from 1950–1957. Interviewed at his home in San Francisco on October 25, 2005.

6 BILL DOLBY, Alcatraz Alumni Association Newsletter 1996.

7 CHUCK STUCKER, island resident from 1940–1943 and from 1948–1953, former Alcatraz Alumni president and noted Alcatraz historian and archivist. Interviewed November 14, 2005.

8 JOLENE BABYAK, *Eyewitness on Alcatraz: True Stories of Families Who Live on the Rock* (Berkeley, Calif.: Ariel Vamp Press, 1996), 20

9 STUCKER, interviewed November 14, 2005, and at his home in Dixon, Calif., on June 6, 2006.

10 MICHAEL ESSLINGER, *Alcatraz: A Definitive History of the Penitentiary Years* (San Francisco: Ocean View Publishing, 2008), 127.

11 STUCKER, spoke with Barbara Johnston at her home a few months before she died.

12 BILL DOLBY, e-mail dated February 8, 2006.

13 CLIFFORD FISH, guard on Alcatraz from 1938–1962. Videotaped interview held in the Alcatraz archives of Chuck Stucker. Viewed on April 1, 2008.

14 FREDERICK R. BECHDOLT, *"The Rock,"* Saturday Evening Post (November 2, 1935), 5.

15 FRANK J. TAYLOR, *"Alcatraz: Pen for the Toughest,"* Colliers, (July 25, 1936), 11.

16 JAMES A. JOHNSTON, *Alcatraz Island Prison: And the Men Who Live There* (Douglas/Ryan Communication, 1999), 44.

17 ESSLINGER, *Alcatraz,* 141

18 ROBERT J. SCHOENBERG, *Mr. Capone: The Real—and Complete—Story of Al Capone* (New York: Quill/William Morrow, 1992), 332.

19 JOHNSTON, *Alcatraz Island Prison,* 40

20 ESSLINGER, *Alcatraz,* 144

21 MARK DOUGLAS BROWN, *Capone: Life Behind Bars at Alcatraz* (San Francisco: Golden Gate National Parks Conservancy, 2004) 35. Letter from convict #97 to Al Capone's brother, Ralph.

22 PHYLLIS (HESS) TWINNEY lived on Alcatraz Island from 1934–1939. Interviewed by phone on December 6, 2005.

23 STUCKER, interviewed April 1, 2008.

24 FISH, videotaped interview held in the Alcatraz archives of Chuck Stucker. Viewed on April 1, 2008.

25 http://www.toothbrushexpress.com/html/floss_history.html

26 MARILYN TOWER OLIVER, *Alcatraz Prison in American History* (Berkeley Heights, N.J.: Enslow Publishers, 1998)

27 Alcatraz Alumni Newsletter, July 1993.

ACKNOWLEDGMENTS

This book would not have been possible without the help of so many people who have generously shared with me details of their lives growing up on Alcatraz Island. Most especially Chuck and his lovely wife, Leta, who allowed me to park in their living room for days on end combing the amazing Alcatraz archives Chuck has compiled. George DeVincenzi, who has a wonderful memory and many crisp and colorful stories about his life as a guard on Alcatraz Island. Rocky Chandler for writing his book *Alcatraz, the Hard Years* and for allowing me to "shake the hand that shook the hand of Al Capone." Jolene Babyak, Sharon Haller, Ed Faulk, Phyllis "Sweetie" Hess Twinney, and the late Clifford Fish, whose stories about his twenty-four years working as a guard on Alcatraz—as videotaped by Chuck Stucker—were truly amazing. I would also like to thank Darwin Coons, ex–bank robber, for answering my questions about what it was like to be behind bars on Alcatraz.

A special thanks go to my team of expert readers: Peter Seraichick, Dr. Douglas Ellison, Dr. Shelley Hwang, Chuck Stucker, Michael Esslinger, Phyllis "Sweetie" Hess Twinney for their help with the text. They all provided me with expertise I don't have, but all mistakes are definitely mine and mine alone.

A heartfelt thanks to my editor, Kathy Dawson for sticking by me through thick and thin, good drafts and bad ones. Editing me is sort of like trying to put a seat belt on the Energizer Bunny and Kathy always manages to make it look effortless. I would like to thank Betsy Groban and Jen Haller of Houghton Mifflin Harcourt and Lauri Hornik of Dial and my agent, Elizabeth Harding, of Curtis, Brown for their graciousness in all things.

And most of all I would like to thank the many many teachers in the United States and in the United Kingdom who have taught *Al Capone Does My Shirts* in their classrooms. It is your work that has brought my book to life for your students and I will always be indebted to you.